LIVE ALBUM REVIEW

BY EDWARD MILANO

Live Album Review

No part of this book is to be reproduce, or stored in a retrieval system, or transmitted in any form or photocopying, recording, or otherwise without express written permission of the publisher.

Copyright© Edward Milano 2024

Cover Art/ llustrations by Chloe Brogan

ISBN: 979-8-3303-0313-7

Live Album Review

To those searching for the lost chord, the eternal note, and are gratefully captivated in the

music of the spheres. Those who recognize the healing power of music and have captured,

trained and gladly released it with sounds from the lyre, harp and ram's horn. This book is for

you.

Thank you.

Edward Milano

TABLE OF CONTENTS

INTRODUCTION 7

ON THE ROAD 11

LIVE AND DANGEROUS 14

GET YER YA-YA'S OUT! 16

LIVE! BOOTLEG 21

IF YOU WANT BLOOD 23

(YOU'VE GOT IT) 23

AN EVENING WITH JOHN DENVER 25

LIVE! IN THE AIR AGE 28

ON YOUR FEET OR ON YOUR KNEES 33

BEFORE THE FLOOD 37

LIVE! 41

AT BUDOKAN 45

CHICAGO (LIVE!) 47

LIVE! 49

FROM MADISON SQUARE GARDEN 49

ROYAL ALBERT HALL LONDON 52

MAY 2-3-4-5-6 52

FOUR WAY STREET 56

MADE IN JAPAN 61

WELCOME BACK MY FRIENDS TO THE SHOW
THAT NEVER ENDS-LADIES AND GENTLEMEN
64

17-11-10 68

LIVE! RAISIN' HELL 71

LIVE! 73

FRAMPTON COMES ALIVE! 75

LIVE! 79

SPACE RITUAL 81

PERFORMANCE ROCKIN' 86

THE FILLMORE 86

RUNNING ON EMPTY 89

MAD DOGS AND ENGLISHMEN 92

YOU CAN'T ARGUE WITH 97

A SICK MIND 97

AT SAN QUENTIN 99

KISS ALIVE! 101

THE SONG REMAINS THE SAME 103

LEON LIVE! 108

WAITING FOR COLUMBUS 113

LIVE! DEAD 117

Live Album Review

ROCK AND ROLL ANIMAL	121
ONE MORE FROM THE ROAD	123
KICK OUT THE JAMS	125
LIVE!	130
DELIVERIN'	133
JOURNEY TO THE CENTER OF THE EARTH	135
EXIT STAGE LEFT	137
THE GOLDEN AGE OF	139
ROCK AND ROLL	139
LIVE!	141
ALIVE IN AMERICA	147
BRING ON THE NIGHT	150
BROTHER BAND AT FILMORE EAST	152
LIVE! AT THE BBC	155
CONCERT FOR BANGLADESH	157
IT'S ALIVE	165
LIVE AT LEEDS	168
AROUND THE WORLD WITH THREE DOG NIGHT	169
WINGS OVER AMERICA	172
YESSONGS	176
ZAPPA/MOTHERS ROXY AND	183

ELSEWHERE	183
YARDBIRDS FIVE LIVE!	186
IT'S TOO LATE TO STOP NOW	190
LIVE! AT SUNBURY	192
BLOW OUT YOUR FACE	197
FULL HOUSE	199
THE APOLLO THEATRE PRESENTS IN PERSON THE JAMES BROWN SHOW	201
LIVE! IN CONCERT	205
LIVE!	209
RAUNCH AND ROLL LIVE	212
LIVE! AT WOODSTOCK	215
GRAND FUNK LIVE!	220
LIVE! AFTER DEATH	225
BURSTING OUT	228
U.S.A	232
LIVE! RUST	234
STRANGER IN THIS TOWN	239
HOT AUGUST NIGHT	241
RAINBOW ON STAGE	244
LIVE!	247
ALOHA FROM HAWAII	251

Edward Milano

FREE LIVE!	257
LIVE! BULLET!	259
BAND OF GYPSIES	261
ALIVE SHE CRIED	265

INTRODUCTION

Neil Young wrote, "'Live music is better', bumper stickers should be issued." in his song Union Man.

David Crosby explained the pressure of Crosby, Stills, Nash and Young with a critic's question "Good record, good record, but can you do it live?"

These quotes guide my mind-set regarding a musical artist's talent.

Can they do it in a live setting without a safety net?

A few years ago, I was going through a painful time in my personal life. I found myself keeping busy by doing cathartic DIY construction around my empty house. I found myself sharing it with two dogs and four cats. Since the house was void of any other human occupants, I had the freedom to blast music as loud as I wanted. I loved that aspect of living alone because I could dig out any album in my extensive collection that other people couldn't tolerate; especially at extreme volume. I gravitated toward music that I loved and listened to when I was a teenager, when life seemed simpler. This created a tidal wave of emotions, long buried and finally surfacing. It was life-giving allowing me to take hope in this truth: that something good can come from something bad. I discovered that an artist's live albums were more enjoyable to me than their studio ones. I realized *Made in Japan*, a live recording, was better listening than *Machine Head* studio album. Both performed by Deep Purple; what was the difference? Then *One More from the Road* was better than *Second Helping* both by Lynyrd Skynyrd. *Rock and Roll Animal* was greater than *Berlin* both by Lou Reed. This made me consider the possibilities of this personal revelation. Live recording was better than in studio albums. I like to think that over the decades, I have learned a thing or two about music.

I like to write creatively and with the formats offered by Facebook. I can operate a page that will allow me to share my thoughts with fellow music lovers around the world. I could focus on live albums and go from there. I released the *Live Album Review* to the world.

After a couple years of cranking out live album reviews, a respected friend who faithfully read my page suggested I put some of my reviews in book form. A book? That seemed a bit of a stretch. Bob Dylan wrote books. Who am I? Who would pay good money to read my drivel? My friend seemed confident it would work.

After exhausting every excuse to not do it. As you can read, I did it. I really did it and hope you enjoy it. It's only my opinion, it's only rock and roll, with a little humor sprinkled on top.

Live Album Review

ON THE ROAD

BY: TRAFFIC

On The Road, now that's a live album that was owned and operated by many in an 'altered state'. I always thought they should have called the album DUI, but I doubt the record company would have signed off on that. Released in 1973, it was originally a single LP, containing four songs *Glad/Freedom Rider, Tragic Magic, (Sometimes I feel so) Uninspired,* and *Shoot Out at The Fantasy Factory*. This type of album, designed for people to light up and enjoy, featured extended jams like Glad (21:00) as the norm.

It didn't take long to realize one album just wasn't enough. The double album, reissued on CD, made more sense for the people that liked Traffic's unique noise and the core members of Stevie Winwood, Jim Capaldi and Chris Wood.

"Glad/Freedom Rider" opened this set from Germany. It's not much different from the studio version, other than the drawn-out sax voicing from Chris Wood. By the time

Live Album Review

they had finished with *"Freedom Rider,"* twenty minutes had transpired. Not that anyone really noticed. Who would complain anyway? We were too busy staring at the album cover and watching it move.

Tragic Magic follows, and it's an instrumental that Chris Wood breaks out his flute on. Eight minutes is short for a song on this set, but that's more than enough time. The unsung heroes here are the backing musicians. Barry Beckett on piano and organ, David Hood on bass, and Roger Hawkins on drums are all *Muscle Shoals* (a separate album by Traffic) vets whose solid accompaniment allows the 'Big Three' to wander, meander, and even drive erratically without crashing or going into a ditch. Anthony "Rebop" Kwaku Baahwas there on percussion as well and sometimes it's hard to distinguish his flavors from Jim Capaldi's work.

Sometimes *"I Feel So Uninspired"* is over ten minutes of Stevie Winwood's soulful voice and his excellent lead guitar playing. *"Shoot Out At The Fantasy Factory"* is the title track from the studio album they were touring behind and it clocks in at over seventeen minutes and everyone, even the backing band members, contributed.

Again, remembering listening to this while sitting with a group after passing the bong was a trip. Not necessarily down memory lane, but a trip nonetheless. It's phenomenal music that doesn't need dissecting for its progressive jazz/

rock flows and is good for 'the head,' as was the lingo.

"Light Up Or Leave Me Alone" is the only song Capaldi sings and its eleven minutes are the closest to rock as this set gets. Stevie again displays his guitar work, and it's surprising at how accomplished he is.

"Low Spark Of High Heeled Boys" finishes this album (does anyone but me wonder why these guys insisted on such long song titles?) and it's almost eighteen minutes of minimalist sax and piano improvisation, over the cool, laid-back groove. It takes off about half-way through and the band wakes up before bringing it home.

The only issue, 40 years ago, when somebody noticed the music stopped, was who was going to get up and put another album on.

When *On The Road* was first released, the critics criticized it for being boring and self-indulgent. I think it was perfect for that time in history when people indulged and did boring things like sit around and listen to music. After decades have passed, it still stands up today as a classic live album from Traffic remains enjoyable with or without the help of controlled substances.

LIVE AND DANGEROUS

BY: THIN LIZZY

LIVE AND DANGEROUS is a double live album from Thin Lizzy, released in 1978. These guys could never break into the American market, unfortunately. I guess The Boss (Bruce Springsteen) was more than enough for those *Born in the USA.* Phil Lynott, the lead singer, bass player and principal songwriter, was the focal point. His songs are hard rock, Van Morrison style. If you listen to *"Dancing In the Moonlight"*, you'll see why. That, and the beautiful heart wrenching ballad, *"Still In Love With You"*, are the stand-outs.

Just about everything else, including, *"The Boys Are Back in Town"*, is the tried-and-true Thin Lizzy f ormula. Excellent guitar work from Brain Robertson and Scott Gorham (those dudes were the real rock stars) a surplus of hummable Riffage and dual melodic leads. Tight and exceptional drumming from Brain Downey; all a vehicle for Lynott's voice. Most of the songs would have been excellent instrumentals.

Lynott's singing is more impassioned, speaking with

a serviceable chorus, delivered with the cadence and style as Bruce Springsteen. The similarities are too noticeable to ignore. I'm not sure who came first, Bruce or Phil, but what is undeniable is that both of them attended Van Morrison High School. I would give the nod to Phil Lynott because of the Irish connection. Listening to this album, you feel that Phil Lynott is a man trying to serve two masters.

A sensitive poet, locked into an image and musical form that he so desperately wants to get away from. Few introspective songs of his make the cut here for this is a rock band playing for an audience of people who came for that. How much is authentic, live music? According to band members, they recorded at least 25% of it in a studio.

It matters very little, just for the song, "Still in Love With You," the band could have played the phone book and this album would be worth having. One item worth mention-ing is that Huey Lewis (yes, that Huey Lewis and the News.) plays harmonica on the 12-bar blues, *Baby Drives Me Crazy*". At the time he was in the band Clover, who was a supporting act to Thin Lizzy. I bet you didn't know that.

Live Album Review

GET YER YA-YA'S OUT!

BY: THE ROLLING STONES

With an album title taken from a Blind Boy Fuller song by the same name. The inspiration for the cover photo came from the Dylan song *"Visions of Johanna,"* leading to the question whether The Rolling Stones in 1970 had anything original to give anymore. That, or they were saying, "this entire album is a rip-off." Guess what boys, and girls, it's not. For my money, *Get Yer Ya-Ya's Out!* I believe it is the best of all The Rolling Stones live albums.

From the opening song *"Jumping Jack Flash"* to the concluding tune *"Street Fighting Man"* the Stones play as if they have something to prove. At the time, they actually did. This was their first American tour in three years, one that a rock critic had labeled a "mythic rock and roll tour." They were also breaking in Brian Jones's replacement, a young 20-year-old former The Bluesbreaker named Mick Taylor. This album is, of course, history. From our present vantage point, but back then it was a gamble. I still enjoy listening to it decades after its release because the band reinvented themselves into dangerous friends of the devil.

Basically, they were starting over. They didn't have The Beatles to follow and tap for creativity anymore. By attrition, they were forced to lead the charge and settled into a hard rocking, American blues based sound. It's still the Stones, but there's a darkness surrounding the music.

The Richards/Taylor interplay would serve them well for the next few years, in my opinion, their best period musically. The way they play *"Honky Tonk Women"* is so ugly it hurts, but it hurts so good. This is where you can find the ultimate version of *"Midnight Rambler,"* where Mick Taylor gets the opportunity to introduce himself to the world. Mick Jagger performs it as if pure evil possessed him. I wonder, at this period, if he was acting at all. Yes, many versions of this song exist but this one is the only one that captures the darkness of the band..

Of course, the record label has released updated anniversary editions of this album that contain more tunes and opening act sets. Go ahead, smoke 'em if ya got 'em.

I like the well worn, scratchy vinyl album of this. It's sinister. It still makes me feel like I'm doing something wrong. After handling the record, I feel like I need to wipe sulfur residue off my fingers. The music playing gives the sensa-

Live Album Review

tion of opening a hole to hell. Considering the murder at the Altamont show happened only a few weeks after this live recording took place, I would surmise the boys did indeed "play with fire."

Edward Milano

LIVE! BOOTLEG

BY: AEROSMITH

I liked Aerosmith back in the seventies, Toxic Twins was a well-earned nickname for Steven Tyler and Joe Perry. They put out some excellent music and were running on drugs, booze, and bagels. In 1978, Aerosmith released *LIVE! BOOTLEG*, featuring songs from their first 5 studio albums, including *"Come Together"* from Sgt. Pepper's Lonely Hearts Club Band movie. They include the ones I like too, which is a bonus: *"Walk This Way"*, *"Sweet Emotion"*, *"Dream On"* and *"Back in the Saddle"*. When they get funky with *"Last Child"* I keep expecting David Bowie to jump in and sing *"Fame"*. They even do an early version of *"Chip Away"*, which is one of my all-time favorite Aerosmith tunes. I never made the connection before, but early Guns and Roses sure sound like early Aerosmith. If Axl Rose was singing the vocals instead of Steve Tyler, I'd dare you to not agree. The production values sound more like a soundboard recording, but I guess that's why they called it *LIVE! BOOTLEG*.

The guitars definitely stand out, enhancing the clarity of Joe Perry's skills, which surpass those of most hard rock guitarists who copied his style. I must admit I dusted this one off before playing, but it was an enjoyable trip down memory lane when I actually thought Aerosmith's music was good. I don't want to make light of substance abuse and addiction, a serious struggle for many artists from this era. We can't deny, though, how their altered-mind state affected their music. Why, sometimes did an artists best music happen when they were in an altered state?

Live Album Review

IF YOU WANT BLOOD (YOU'VE GOT IT)

BY: AC/DC

When I listen to AC/ DC I have to turn off my brain. This is genital rock. *IF YOU WANT BLOOD (YOU'VE GOT IT)* was released in 1978 and it features 'the' Bon Scott on lead vocals, who passed shortly after in 1980 from alcohol poisoning a consequence of the 'Drugs and Rock n' Roll' era. The band was just starting to make some inroads into America. Then Mutt Lange's later help would become huge for their growth. Forget that they rewrote every song on this album time and time again.

Malcom and Angus Young were pint-sized geniuses at reworking classic guitar riffs, all in the same key. This live set, reportedly from Glasgow, is loud, rebellious, nasty and a whole lotta fun. Bon Scott tells his tales, singing in a voice that sounds like he swallowed razor blades. Phil Rudd and Cliff Williams are a tight and steady rhythm section, keeping everything simple while Malcolm and Angus Young are in their own little world of ax mastery. Angus is a skilled player and always managed to pull off a distinct solo, with complete control of his tone. The song, *"Riff Raff"* is first on this album and it's typical of what made AC/DC work for their fans. Fast maximum volume songs, rooted in the blues with riffs that are easily understood.

Great tunes are on this album: *"Whole Lotta Rosie"*, *"High Voltage"*, *"The Jack"* and *"Let There Be Rock"*. All of those sung, tongue-in-cheek by Bon Scott. Musically, it grooves but the visual action is necessary to get the full impact of AC/DC's live act. Angus Young's insanity, wearing his school boy outfit, occasionally mooning the crowd, Bon Scott's charismatic, sinister presence, and the coolness of the rest of the band. It taps perfectly into the teenage male, testosterone fueled psyche of, "I don't care and will punch out anyone who tries to mess with me and my good time."

What more can you ask for? Get wasted, turn off your brain, get out your air guitar and bang your head.

Live Album Review

AN EVENING WITH JOHN DENVER

BY: JOHN DENVER

Before 'Americana' was a vogue coinage, there was John Denver. In 1975, he had a few hit songs and was fast becoming the contemporary artist that even your parents liked. That reason alone made many teenage guys take an immediate dislike to him. Despite being considered too straight by the rock stars of the day, they still respected him. Anyone who pens a song like *"Leaving On A Jet Plane"* can't be all bad. Pete Townsend has said he appreciated John Denver's songwriting. John Lennon, in a roundabout way, insulted Paul by comparing his guitar work on the song *"Blackbird"* to John Denver. It's interesting to me that Paul's song, *"Mother Nature's Son"* makes an appearance here, so I would guess John Denver is a McCartney apologist.

AN EVENING WITH JOHN DENVER's release signaled the beginning of a new chapter in his career, establishing his lasting presence. All 23 songs on this double album are stand- alone performances, with brilliant arrangements and musicianship. Like him or not, if you were around during this time, you either had the album, knew someone that did, or heard songs from it on the radio. Try as you might, you could not escape its charm.

Recorded from a series of shows at the Universal Amphitheatre in L.A. in 1974, John has a great backing band that includes Steve Weisberg and John Somers, who compliment him with a myriad of stringed instruments. Hal Blaine is here too. That guy showed up everywhere, it seemed, and for good reason. He could do it all on drums and percussion without wrecking things. There's an orchestra on stage and at first you wonder if it's necessary until they join in on "*The Eagle*" and "*The Hawk*". John stretches the limits of his voice at the end but still pulls it off. Every time I hear it, I can feel the struggle and I sigh in relief when it ends. That's the only tune with any hint of tension, for everything else is pastoral, optimistic and joyful, that you, as a listener, want to grin from ear-to-ear, just like John is doing on the front cover. You are more than ready to book a flight to the Colorado Rocky Mountains pronto. West Virginia's Blue Ridge Mountains would come in a close second.

The songs of "*Grandma's Feather Bed*", "*Thank God I'm A Country Boy*", "*Rocky Mountain High*", "*Take Me Home Country Roads*", "*Sweet Surrender*" and "*Rocky Mountain Suite*" are enough to make for a stellar show but he also

Live Album Review

dedicates two songs to his wife, one to his guitar, one to his home and one to the city of Toledo, Ohio. I doubt today he would have included the last line about the ladies and dogs, but that was then and things weren't as PC sensitive in the 'wild 70s.' You have to take into account that John Denver's live album was up against the live albums of KISS, Peter Frampton and Loggins and Messina.

He needed a bit of an edge, so "*Saturday Night in Toledo, Ohio*" was him stepping away from the 'nice guy' image and taking it to the underbelly of the dirty metropolis. His street cred significantly shot up and that may have been what sent this album over the top. I'm just funnin' with ya. "Far Out."

LIVE! IN THE AIR AGE

BY: BE BOP DELUXE

A live album from the 1970s was almost a guaranteed good listen. Many live albums were also the only album from an artist worth having. I can't say that about Be Bop Deluxe, which released some great studio albums. The live set, *Live! In The Air Age*, from 1977, is about as perfect a live album can be. It has great songs, brilliant performances and a great sound. They surely designed it with care to generate more interest in the band and hopefully accomplish for them what *Frampton Comes Alive!* did for Peter Frampton. It didn't and there's not enough time or space to list all the reasons.

Space is a perfect description of this album anyway, so focusing on that is more fun. Bill Nelson, the architect of the flying saucer Be Bop Deluxe, landed his craft periodically in the 1970s and left the inhabitants of Earth with some of his futuristic sounds and musings. He crafted this excellent live album of concert delights that was originally packaged with two white vinyl albums (one a regular LP and the other an

Live Album Review

EP).

To call Bill Nelson "seminal," is almost an insult. He was original and way, way ahead of his time in sound, concept and visual presentation. Those who liked and were influenced by him, took bits and pieces of his total vision and used them to create their own style and music. Artists like New Wave, 80s David Bowie, Adrian Belew, Talking Heads, and The Cars, just to name a few, were heavily influenced by Be Bop Deluxe and took generous and almost criminal helpings from his total vision to create their own style and music. Include some blazing, innovative guitar mastery with progressive rock elements and you are starting to scratch the surface of Bill Nelson and Be Bop Deluxe.

LIVE! IN THE AIR AGE works as a document, an introduction and a souvenir. Whoever hears it, fan or unfamiliar alike, will be changed. That's the mission and one look at the album cover, from the groundbreaking, silent film, 'Metropolis,' is a clue that Be Bop Deluxe is beyond having, "a good beat and I can dance to it," mentality from Dick Clark's American Bandstand. It's challenging, impressive and modern.... even today. You can dance if you want to.

A wash of effects, that sounds like a space vessel arriving, begins each side of each album. That same effect occurs, as if the same ship is taking off at the conclusion of each side. That's cool, man. The music offered is alternate reality songs, played by stellar musicians. Each song is full of hooks, key changes, tempo fluctuations and dynamic inter-facing. Cherry-picked songs are selected, with less embel-lishment than their studio counterparts, to feature the gen-uine quality and the amazing ability of the musicians to play them.

Charlie Tumahai on bass, Simon Fox on drums and Cabasa El Dubova on percussion are a precise rhythm sec-tion that operates in a time/space continuum; they basically are the engine section of the spacecraft. While Andrew Clark on keyboards, Bill Nelson on guitar and vocals are the navi-gator and captain. They play ten helpings of excellence and if there ever was a live album from the 70s that "should have been, " it's this one.

To dissect every song would require cryosleep. The shorter numbers are mini operas, with enough ideas to baffle a space cadet.It's the voyages into deep space that take this album into interstellar overdrive. Let's not mistake this band for Pink Floyd. It's not trippy music- it's rock music played sideways.

"*Adventures in a Yorkshire Landscape*" is a mellow atmosphere that evokes a myriad of emotions. The interplay between the guitar and keyboards is what Major Tom would listen to as he's taking a protein pill. When a solo spacewalk occurs, it reminds you of some incredible performances you

Live Album Review

may have heard somewhere else by someone else. Who are these guys? Who is this incredible guitarist? Is Frank Zappa in the house? How about Gary Moore? No.....it's all Bill Nelson. When Andrew Clark and his keyboard returns to normal gravity, Bill calls out his name (I think that's what he's saying). He's not saying, "Bob Mayo."

The instrumental of *"Shine"* is a bright star in the heavenly expanse. Jeff Beck has got nothing on this funky jazz fusion. It's a reality based space jam with lead boots on the ground. I think it's a Bill Nelson extravaganza. "You want a guitar? Here, have some guitar." It just reinforces the bias of the music industry. Why isn't he mentioned in the same sentence as those other guitar godz? Maybe he is, but in a different dimension. People just don't give him as much recognition in this one.

I recommend anyone who likes classic rock to recognize this album. It's a great one and if contact with extraterrestrials happens in your lifetime, then you may have something in common.

Edward Milano

Live Album Review

ON YOUR FEET OR ON YOUR KNEES

BY: BLUE OYSTER CULT

The Master of Ceremonies, from this 1975 live album *On Your Feet or On Your Knees*, introduces the band as "The amazing Blue Oyster Cult."

I'm not sure about "amazing" but they are pretty good. This album sold well, and it covered their first three albums, which were probably their best three albums too. There's no point in discussing this band's philosophy and if they were or were not America's answer to Black Sabbath. I will just say they were too cerebral for the majority of their audience. Music critics from the self-proclaimed important music publications weren't too kind. I guess they could overlook the comic book, Sci-Fi and even the occult topics, but subtle references to The Third Reich were another matter entirely. They didn't look and act like tree-hugging rock stars. No, they preferred to swim in the underground's sweat (cool lyrics, if I say so myself). They didn't care if you O.D.'d on life itself. They weren't doing it to make friends with you. They don't even like you, unless your face looks like a foot. Atypical love songs were devoted to vampires or Canadian Huskies. They didn't champion drugs, but spun tales of drug deals gone bad.

Musically, their individual songs contained more ideas than most bands' albums. They certainly demonstrate that here too. Some of their tunes are complex enough to give many pro-rockers a run for their money, but this band was all about the boogie. Call them Steppenwolf's kid brothers and they even play, *"Born to Be Wild"*. People familiar with this band will recognize *"Cities On Flame"*, *"Subhuman"*, *"Hot Rails To Hell"*, *"Last Days Of May"*, *"The Red and The Black"*, *"Harvester Of Eyes"*, *"A Recap and 7 Screaming Dizbusters"*, that all work well in an arena full of drunken masses. The song, *"Buck's Boogie"* is a formula stealing, crowd pleasing, instrumental, sucked from the veins of Deep Purple. It's a tried-and-true formula, and if you can pull it off, then more power to you. Blue Oyster Cult pulls it off, you Transmani-acon.

Buck Dharma is the greatest ignored guitarist in rock. Either he wasn't interested in the acclaim or too vertically challenged (you pick) but he is a Godzilla. Alan Lanier on keyboards is ever present without being overbearing, as if he were a veteran of a psychic war. The Bouchard brothers hold down the rhythm duties while Eric Bloom does what he does. Hey, he announces from the stage that he's on a first

Live Album Review

name basis with the devil and that he calls him "Lou." Whatever you say Eric.

The song *"Maserati"* sounds more like "The Motor City Madman" and it is a barnburner. Here, Blue Oyster Cult takes flight and they are jam-up and jelly-tight. I'm not sure, but I think that's the section of their show where everyone, including the drummer, and that guy 'Lou', play guitar. It's like a military parade formation, with everyone holding a guitar, lined up and wailing away. I most like that they insert the riff to *"L.A. Woman"* and on the first attempt at replicating the dual harmony of the guitar passage, they mess it up. It's so noticeable it's funny and guess what? Baby Ice Dog. They left it on the album. Now that's live music without a net. It must be mentioned that Blue Oyster Cult incorporated bombs blowing up, a light show, fog, flash pots, and lasers into their act. This, of course, is not available in this format, but it doesn't matter. In many cases, a band's stage theatrics covered their crappy music.

The music here stands by itself and I didn't once hear a cowbell, unless 'Lou' was somewhere in the ether, playing a silent clang and keeping time, that only the band members could hear. If so, I didn't hear it because I roll with Jesus, but I can hear the sounds from Blue Oyster Cult, loud and clear. "Know thine enemy," I guess, is another way of saying, "I like this music and don't think the gates of hell are opening up to drag me in."

BEFORE THE FLOOD

BY: BOB DYLAN/ THE BAND

Bob Dylan/The Band's *Before the Flood* is one of the most famous collaborations in rock history. The double album is a true meeting of trusted friends, at a halfway house, where they can be themselves and slowly get their act together. Dylan was entering the 70s, energized and reinventing himself. The Band already had a great reputation but was in a state of flux. Together, Dylan and The Band were able to help each other while creating some splendid music. "*Planet Waves*" didn't set the planet on fire but was an excellent return to form by Dylan and a time for The Band to relax and ponder, "What's next?"

Bob Dylan said, during the tour, that he was playing at being Bob Dylan. He didn't consider this a high water mark in his legacy, even though he is singing and playing as if he has something to prove. The album title isn't some prophetic warning, but a sarcastic take on the flood of bootlegs from this tour that was guaranteed to follow.

Live Album Review

Dylan breaks up the sections in the live set to rework well-known songs from his back pages, while The Band is content to play some of their greatest hits. The Forum in Los Angeles is the scene where this music took place and the 1974 release would be Bob Dylan's first official live album.

"*Most Likely You Go Your Way and I'll Go Mine*" is the opener. It sounds as if Dylan is informing his audience that he isn't an idealistic kid anymore. He is a jaded survivor that is bruised and torn. The performance is far from a weary tune. It's clear, direct and with The Band's accompaniment, it rolls like a noisy, speeding train that you better hold on tight to or it will leave you in the dust. Dylan is saying, without question, that this is who he is now, while pointing in the direction he's headed. If you don't like it, then get your "boot hills a wandering". "*Lay Lady Lay*", "*Rainy Day Women*", "*Knockin' on Heaven's Door*", "*It Ain't Me Babe*" and "*Ballad of a Thin Man*" are each given special treatment by The Band, who interpret the songs as if they wrote them. This gives Bob Dylan the freedom to sing with a new passion and fresh voice, giving a different meaning to the originals.

The Band took it from there and do, "*Up On Cripple Creek*", "*I Shall Be Released*", "*Endless Highway*", "*The Night They Drove Old Dixie Down*" and "*Stage Fright*". They could have carried the show by themselves but they are seasoned and professional enough to do their stuff with enough respect to not show up The Boss.

Bob does acoustic readings of, *"Don't Think Twice It's Alright"*, *"Just Like a Woman"* and *"It's Alright Ma, I'm Only Bleeding.'* With just his voice, guitar and harmonica, he's vulnerable and alone. His folk days had him in this same scene, playing this same part. Here he's a different actor, with a different motivation. He can still hold a crowd, only the songs take on a different life by the way he spits the lyrics and the way he makes his guitar and harmonica speak.

The Band does *"The Shape I'm In"*, *"When You Awake"* and *"The Weight"* with the same gusto as their previous set. This group shows how five individual and creative souls can work together to form a masterpiece. Imagine having them as a backing band.

Dylan has them as a backing band for he joins them on reworking, *"All Along the Watchtower"*, *"Highway 61 Revisited"*, *"Like a Rolling Stone"* and *"Blowin' In the Wind"*. There are different flavors than you're accustomed to tasting and different noises than you're used to hearing. These four songs would make the career of anyone else but are just part of a long list in Dylan's playbook. The picture of the flames, held up by the individuals in the crowd, on the album cover is us saying, "Give us more." Dylan would, but not with The Band. That was what we hoped was going to happen and the two entities would go through the rest of the 1970s playing together. We didn't know it would be a Last Waltz.

LIVE!

BY: BOB MARLEY AND THE WAILERS

It was the year 1975. I was having a conversation with someone, I don't remember who, about music. "Hey, man. You ever heard of Bob Marley?"

"No."

"He's the dude that wrote that Eric Clapton song, 'I Shot the Sheriff.'"

"So?"

In the immortal words of Al Czervk, "So let's dance."

Dance is what this famous of famous live albums makes you do. From the opening song, "*Trenchtown Rock*", the reggae groove is non-stop for over 37 minutes. Yes...37 minutes. Skimpy by today's standards, but this album, *LIVE!*, dropped in 1975, was intended as an introduction to America. A short LP record meant the sound quality would be great. That engineering decision was successful because the music is warm and inviting. Every instrument is distinct, and every voice is clear. It allowed the space needed for the music to breathe.

All songs are from a concert in London. The Brits had already discovered Marley's genius, and the audience showed it by cheering at every song's introduction and singing along to choruses. Today, these tunes are considered classics, but at the time of its release, most people in America were just getting hip.

This live album is one of those 'feel good' memories. *"No Woman, No Cry"*, *"I Shot the Sheriff"*, *"Lively Up Yourself"* and *"Get Up, Stand Up"* were life changing when I heard them for the first time at 17 years old. I was hooked. The Wailers could play. The 'I Threes' could sing. Bob Marley was, without question, an original. Name a song that you have to stop what you're doing and listen with good intentions? *"No Woman, No Cry"* from this set is one of those. I didn't shoot the sheriff, but I am guilty of letting Bob Marley's music take priority over adult responsibility.

Live Album Review

AT BUDOKAN

BY: CHEAP TRICK

This album, released domestically in 1979, was originally never intended for American ears. Cheap Trick, at the time, was just a novelty act. They had outstanding success in Japan, hence the *AT BUDOKAN* album. An influx of imports made the record company release it stateside and as a result, Cheap Trick became a household name. The early hits are here, "*Surrender, Ain't That a Shame*" and "*I Want You to Want Me*".

I was always disappointed that they didn't extend the opening song, "*Hello There*". As soon as the band hits that rocking groove, they abruptly end it.

"*Need Your Love*" is the showstopper and Robin Zander sings very creepily. The majority of the crowd is very young teenage girls and knowing that fact, he comes off more of a pervert than a nice boy from Illinois. Were Cheap Trick nice boys? The band's name itself should be food for thought. It's still delightful music and allowed this band to

Live Album Review

break into an area that was traditionally reserved for only teen-beat groups.

Their songs were short, full of hooks and hummable. Robin Zander (the man of a million voices) and Tom Peterson were good looking. Rick Neilson and Bun E. Carlos were goofy looking nerds. This duality served them well.

They did their homework and played music flavored more toward The Beatles than The Stones. They knew Beatle type music was more difficult to pull off and Beatle fans all appreciated it. Besides playing at Nippon Budokan, where The Beatles were the first musical act to ever play there, is kind of going full circle. The songs themselves are more than pop. They are twisted excursions into the psycho ward. A must own album if you must own at least one album by Cheap Trick.

CHICAGO (LIVE!)

BY: CHICAGO

The band Chicago did a series of shows at Carnegie Hall. This ambitious four record set from 1971 contains performances from that brief residency. Four albums? Who could afford that? They included a huge color poster but still... In my opinion, four albums is a bit much.

The album opens with a couple of marginal songs before Robert Lamm plays some nice improvisational piano that sets up the early hit, *"Does Anybody Really Know What Time It Is?"* The band gets bluesy with an extended version of *"South Carolina Purples"* where Terry Kath shows his guitar skills. *"Questions 67 and 68"* allow Peter Cetera to demonstrate his vocals. *"Sing A Mean Tune Kid"* is a tribute to the fallen rock stars and Kath, again, jams hard over a funky riff. This rock stuff is put on hold when the band performs *"Beginnings"* and they tear it up. One wishes they would have included the percussion fun from the studio version, but they end it with a horn blast. Speaking of the horns, the section of "*It Better End Soon*" features them. During this portion of the show, Lamm, Kath, and Cetera take a back seat and allow the others to demonstrate their talents. "*Ballet For A Girl In Buchannon*" is James Pankow's moment of glory. The suite of songs include "*Make Me Smile*" and "*Colour My World*" which make it even more listenable. "*For Richard And His Friends*" is an unreleased protest song performed by the guys, and it is noteworthy for its musical resemblance to something Frank Zappa would have done. The knock on the presidential administration and the Vietnam War shows just how old this album is and how relevant Chicago was attempting to be. "*25 Or 6 To 4*" followed by the jam of "*I'm A Man*" finishes everything up.

It's a great listen from a young band who were still figuring things out. Talent galore with 4 distinct vocalists (one better than Three Dog Night) a guitarist that could blow out your eardrums, a horn section that was tight and melodic and a main composer with deep substance as well as jazz piano chops. They had some rough edges as well as credibility and I think this period of the band is the best, both musically and attitude wise.

Terry Kath's death really changed their direction. This album is when they were young men, searching for so long to find an answer. I like it.

LIVE! FROM MADISON SQUARE GARDEN

BY: ERIC CLAPTON/STEVIE WINDWOOD

In the year 2009, there was a clarion call for the tribes to gather and celebrate the return of the kings. Two royal leaders of the revolution that occurred some 40 years earlier.

Participants and survivors of the revolution brought their children and, in some cases, their children's children. They received instructions to bring gold and lots of it. Eric Clapton and Stevie Winwood, both did these series of concerts right. *LIVE! FROM MADISON SQUARE GARDEN* are two old friends, playing their music, in front of a crowd of people, who, for most of them, were there from the beginning. The hippy/trippy, yin-yang art graphic on the cover may be too obvious, but maybe they are encouraging you to blaze up before listening, like the old days. The band comprised Eric and Stevie, Willie Weeks on bass, Chris Stainton keyboards and Ian Thomas on drums. This stripped down company is perfect. They provide the necessary background

Live Album Review

arrangements to allow both Eric and Stevie to shine.

The set opens with the Blind Faith song, *"Had to Cry Today"*. Eric and Stevie trade lead guitar runs on this and it's more than enough to bring tears to your eyes. They cover Blind Faith-*"Sleeping In the Ground"*, *"Presence of the Lord"*, *"Well Alright"* and *"Can't Find My Way Home"*. Understandable and expected, since they both were members of that classic, short-lived band, some four decades prior. The real mystery, to me anyway, is how did they decide on what else to play? Together, they have careers that span close to a century and made some incredible music and memories over that time. How did they comprise a set list? Pull song titles out of a hat? Throw darts at a list on the wall? Solicited submissions from peers and fans? Maybe they played what they wanted to. However, they did it, they did it right. There are some Traffic songs: *"Glad, Pearly Queen"*, *"Dear Mr. Fantasy"*, *"No Face, No Name, No Number"*. There's Eric Clapton solo stuff including *"Tell the Truth"*, *"Forever Man"*, *"Little Wing"*, *"After Midnight"*, and *"Cocaine"*. They include some blues, *"Low Down, Double Trouble"* and a slowed down version of *"Voodoo Chile"* which is one of the 'must listens' from this set, *"Them Changes"*, *"Rambling on My Mind"*, and *"Georgia"*. This is one concert where the next song and performance is better than the one before. Both Eric and Stevie are trying too. They seem good for each other. These two artists bring out the best in each other, because of a comfortable friend-

Edward Milano

ship and musical compatibility. My question is why didn't they do more music together over the years? Why did it take so long to reunite? This is worth the gold they demand as tribute.

Live Album Review

ROYAL ALBERT HALL LONDON
MAY 2-3-4-5-6

BY: CREAM

I'm so glad Cream reunited for four shows in 2005 at The Royal Albert Hall which was the venue of their farewell concert in 1968.

Has it been that long? Jack Bruce and Ginger Baker's passing makes this album, *ROYAL ALBERT HALL LONDON MAY 2-3-5-6*, that much sweeter.

They open with, *"I'm So Glad"*. Some brief tuning before the song is a great way to prepare the crowd in eager anticipation.

The performance is tight but loose. The guys know each other's moves and styles, as if they never disbanded. The song's conclusion has Bruce and Clapton singing the chorus in acapella harmony. Baker, who doesn't sing, doesn't need to. He just adds his expressive drumming to the vocalists. How cool is that?

"*Spoonful*" is perfect. Clapton's dirty guitar blues-simple but nasty sounding, with Jack Bruce playing complementary bass lines and dancing up and down the frets when the space allows. His vocals are sharp and with an exclamation point on every word. Ginger is Ginger and his identifying drumming is ever present. How many different versions of this song has Clapton released, in different eras with different musicians?

However many, this version goes straight to the top of the list.

That's just two of the 18 performances on this album. They play songs from their three studio albums. No popular solo stuff, which is fine by me.

Psychedelic trips of "*N.S.U.*", "*Sweet Wine*" and "*We're Going Wrong*". The blues classics of "*Spoonful*", "*Outside Woman Blues*", "*Rollin' And Tumblin*", "*Born Under A Bad Sign*", and "*Crossroads*". The adult contemporary change-ups of "*Stormy Monday*" and "*Sleepy Time Time*". Aren't you glad, "*Sunshine Of Your Love*", "*Politician*", "*White Room*" and "*Deserted Cities Of The Heart*" are here as well? Ginger Baker gets in two of his eccentric numbers, "*Pressed Rat And Warthog*" and the drum solo, "*Toad*".

Of course there are missing classics but who really cares? The dudes obviously decided how to set this show

Live Album Review

up and everyone gets equal billing. What's amazing is how good they sound together, even after a few feuding decades. They all never stopped playing, so their chops are fresh. Not bad for three old guys. The only time they come close to sounding old is when their voices strain to sing parts of "*White Room*" (transposing is acceptable, even for arrogant musicians). I guess that's a reason they were considered the first 'SuperGroup'. Unique and ego driven. Separate voices but disciplined enough to not color outside the lines . What makes it even more enjoyable is that the volume is turned well below the threshold of their hey-day. You can hear the interplay between all three. It's tasty and nobody seems to desire to outplay the others. They fit. When Clapton's soloing, the others add their parts as needed. When Jack Bruce is singing, the others don't get in the way. They sure got this one right. They even elected to minimize the soloing.

In days of yore they would play a song out for 30 minutes. Here, the longest is "*Toad*" at 10 minutes, and that's mostly a drum solo. "*Sunshine*" is around 8 minutes and here they give the masses a quick example of the 'old school' free-form jamming they used to do. That's plenty because there's plenty of good music on this set, served up just the way you like it. I like that they felt the need to name each other after an impressive performance. I think they were doing it as a side joke. We know who you are. Why keep telling us, as if we might forget? I'm so glad they didn't forget how to play the songs.

This album will make certain nobody forgets how special the band was and how glad they made us feel. There's a companion DVD but I'm not interested. I don't need to see what they look like after all this time. I heard the expensive tickets were hard to get and that rock royalty was in attendance. Rich musicians playing a concert for rich people. Back when this music was first created, this would have not been cool. How jaded have we become today that it's accepted as the norm?

Live Album Review

FOUR WAY STREET

BY: CSNY

It's 1971 and Crosby, Stills, Nash and Young released a live album. It was from performances in 1970, and received mixed reviews. Many loved it and those that didn't, well... I think they just expected too much. Today, the music and the performances hold up well. These guys certainly wore their politics on their sleeves. Some artists of the day (Dylan, Zappa) ran away from being advocates for the counterculture. These guys embraced it.

Never mind, two of the four weren't even American citizens but found it in their muse to lend their opinion about current American issues. Musically, there's many individual performances, which make the title, *FOUR WAY STREET*, perfect. They kind of tease you at first by opening the album, with CSNY performing the ending of *"Suite Judy Blue Eyes"*. I guess they figure the version on the Woodstock album is enough. They then introduce their 'good friend,' Neil Young, who they assist with on an acoustic, *"On The Way Home"*.

The guys then do, *"Teach Your Children"*. Nash asks the audience to sing along during the chorus (Wait a minute I paid my money and came here to hear you sing, not the people around me). Crosby and Nash then perform some tunes as a duo, *"Triad"*, *"The Lee Shore"*, *"Chicago"* is the good stuff.

Neil Young has a few solo songs too, *"Cowgirl In The Sand"* and *"Don't Let It Bring You Down"*, *"49 Bye Byes/ For What It's Worth"* and *"Love The One You're With"*. The electric stuff, when all four are together, is the most enjoyable. *"Pre-Road Downs"*, *"Long Time Gone"*, *"Southern Man"*, *"Ohio"* and *"Carry On"*. Steve and Neil trade guitar leads and they jam. Okay, besides good song writing, unique harmonies and anti-establishment fervor, this band could mix it up on stage and do it as well, if not better, than anyone else in rock. The bassist, Calvin Smith and drummer, Johnny Barbata, are exceptional. All vocalists sing with passion and conviction. This is CSNY at its peak. Too bad, they were in-fighting at the time and the band would dissolve. That anger obviously gave them some fury here. You have to wonder how good they would have been if they liked each other. It's a great document of what they were and where they may have gone. Crosby has been quoted that CSNY could have been the next Beatles. I doubt that. Just listening to him try and explain how he writes songs is a great example for anybody to the dangers of drug use. But hey, Nash was in The Hollies, that was a British Invasion band that followed The Beatles.

Live Album Review

Crosby was in The Byrds, whose original sound was inspired from The Beatles' Rickenbacker guitars, during HELP. Stills auditioned to be a Monkee, that sitcom band modeled after The Beatles. Young just kind of dropped in. Moreover, they were already established artists when they came together. The Beatles started as young men. CSNY hated each other after a couple years. The Beatles took at least ten years to hate each other. I guess if there's any comparison to The Beatles it would be this.

CSNY was like The Beatles were in 1969. In fact, the closing number, 'Find The Cost Of Freedom' is nice but brief. After a quick interplay of acoustic guitars, the boys sing with that special vocal blend. It's over before you know it. Kind of reminds one of that closing snippet to ABBEY ROAD. The listener is left asking, "Is that all?"

Edward Milano

Live Album Review

MADE IN JAPAN

BY: DEEP PURPLE

What else can we say about this diamond? Deep Purple recorded and released it at the height of their powers. Truth be told, it was a happy accident. The Blackmore, Gillan, Paice, Glover and Lord line up, that is most revered, originally released this for their Japanese audience. Stores in the Western world couldn't order imports fast enough, so Deep Purple and Warner Brothers did the honorable thing and made it available globally. Good thing for it's the album that catapulted them to the upper echelon of hard rock bands.

Now people could make a case for Deep Purple being better than Led Zeppelin, The Who or Black Sabbath. It also helps to have Ritchie Blackmore, who became an almost overnight sensation. He was already a respected guitarist, but after people heard his work on this album, Blackmore was being mentioned in the same breath as Page, Clapton and Beck. Ian Gillan was no slouch as a vocalist. *JESUS CHRIST SUPERSTAR* is ancient history, but the guy could

Live Album Review

sing better than Ozzy or Daltrey and scream better than Plant. Ian Paice on drums was as busy as Moonie, but with more discipline. What Deep Purple had that the others didn't was Jon Lord, and this debate needs to end.

MADE IN JAPAN is when the planets were in alignment, the heavens opened, and positive vibrations surrounded Deep Purple. It all came together at that moment, and like a high performance engine, all the cylinders were firing in unison.

There isn't an unpleasant note on this set from the opening of *"Highway Star"*, where the band settles into a groove, after a melodic prelude from Jon Lord's organ before attacking and I do stress attacking. In fact, they attack every song on this. Highlights are *"Smoke on the Water"* where the air guitar was born. Blackmore's sweet, blues guitar playing on the break-down of *"Strange Kind Of Woman"* is accompanied by Ian Gillan's voice, chopping heads later. There's the jazzy, progressive rock of *"Lazy"* and with some excellent harmonica play from Gillan. Ian Paice drum solo on *"The Mule"* that goes beyond rock music and is just great musicianship that made everyone sit up and take notice that rock and roll had grown up and even if the older generation hated it, they couldn't deny the talent.

Who could ever forget the blood-curdling screams from Gillan on *"Child in Time?"* You can't, as well as the extended space walk that Jon Lord takes during "*Space Truckin*" The musicianship, from beginning to end, is flawless and if you have the studio versions of these songs, you appreciate the added colors and improvisations that will allow you to make sense of their vision. These guys were the real thing, when they wanted to be, even if the critics hated them. They locked onto a formula that worked and it worked here. Too bad, success, money and ego ended up getting in the way. I would have liked to see this line-up during this time. I saw Purple with Coverdale/Hughes and it was so loud you couldn't hear the music, and I am not exaggerating.

Anyway, I still have the original vinyl album from the 70s. I played that endlessly in my room and yes; I owned an air guitar but graduated to a tennis racket. I was the master of it because of this album. It would be interesting to find out how many 8-tracks of this sold because almost everybody in my social circles had it playing in the car. One other important note is that the sound quality is perfect, and this is before analog and digital technology. I was not pleased when reissues and anniversary editions were released, containing more songs. Why mess with perfection? It was the same beef I had when The Who's *LIVE AT LEEDS* was reissued with added material. No, No, No.

Live Album Review

WELCOME BACK MY FRIENDS TO THE SHOW THAT NEVER ENDS-LADIES AND GENTLEMEN

BY: EMERSON, LAKE & PALMER

In the 1970s, it was not unusual for a musical artist to release a double live album. One reason was that they had a backlog of great material and inspired concert performances that needed documenting. Another reason was to fulfill contractual obligations, so legally, it was like releasing two albums. When a triple live album was released, it was a totally different and ambitious animal. Leon Russell, Yes and Chicago dropped triples that were worthy, even if they sometimes bordered on overindulgence and overkill. In 1974, Emerson, Lake and Palmer released their triple-header, *WELCOME BACK MY FRIENDS TO THE SHOW THAT NEVER ENDS-LADIES AND GENTLEMEN...* as a way to put the finishing touches on their past exploits because they were planning an extended break that would last three years.

If you owned this album, you found out right away, the

inside gatefold had some design flaws. The large silver letters of E.L.P. were pockets to hold each disc. I learned early to not carry the album around so the discs could slip out and onto the floor. That was a major bummer. This became a record one elected not to put on while under the influence. This triple album was not as long-player as you would think when each side averaged 18 minutes of music. Engineers designed vinyl to sound better by avoiding the squeezing of the grooves, which was crucial for quadraphonic sound.

Volumes could be written about the *1973 BRAIN SALAD SURGERY* tour and the expense ELP incurred with a convoy of 18 wheelers to transport musical equipment, lights and special effects to the masses. This didn't bring the respect they desired but more of a backlash that gave punk rock grounds to take root. This set was recorded from a show at the Anaheim Convention Center and ELP is at the top of their game, playing as a cooperative of accomplished musicians. They didn't do anything later, in the studio, to augment the sound, so what you're hearing is what the crowd heard that night.

"*Hoedown*" is the opener and it rocks, in ELP fashion, with the wild synthesizer, locomotive rumble of the rhythm section and speedy runs of the organ. This is ELP playing a song they have played countless times that it wouldn't surprise me if they needed to stifle a yawn.

Live Album Review

"*Jerusalem*" is Greg Lake singing over a majestic accompaniment that's less bombastic and It's short and acts as an introduction of his voice, for the instrumental "*Toccata*" follows, and is arranged to give Carl Palmer's drums an early spotlight. He has some cool, cutting edge effects built into this kit, which looked to have a thousand pieces. You can't see that by hearing this but trust me. Side One is over before you know it.

"*Tarkus*" is up next and it's a long one. So lengthy it fills up two sides of the album. Incredible feat to pull off when you consider it's three people providing all the noises. Keith and his massive keyboard set-up, with that monolith looming large and Carl Palmer's thousand toys. Greg Lake seemed out of place-standing like a GQ cover boy while singing, thumping his bass or playing guitar. You can't see that by hearing this, but trust me. Greg fits in "'*Epitaph*" from his King Crimson days, so that's a delightful addition. When the wild ride of "*Tarkus*" gets to "*Take a Pebble*" Greg uses the calm to perform a solo spot, with his acoustic guitar, on "*Still You Turn Me On*" and "*Lucky Man*" I could have gone for more songs by Greg in this fashion. There wasn't enough time, I suppose, for "*Tarkus*" needed to be completed. I'm so glad they squeezed all the 'Impressions' out of it.

Side Four starts with a piano improvisation from Keith. He is playing a white, grand piano that levitates, with him on the bench, in the midst of this performance. You can't see that by listening to this but trust me. *"Take a Pebble"* was sung again before the guys all came together for a rollicking run through of *"Jeremy Bender"*.

Side Five and Six are devoted to *"Karn Evil 9"*. This is the one where Keith Emerson abuses his organ, over the backdrop of smoke and a blinding light show. Carl Palmer's drums rise during his lengthy solo, which was mind blowing fun at the same time. You can't see that by listening to this, but trust me. The visual was an important part of the show and a 'show' is what ELP was giving the U.S.A., as if it was a traveling circus. The music is what really mattered, and they did it in fine, virtuoso fashion. People who witnessed any shows from this tour will testify how well the spectacle worked with the musical performance.

I only described some elements to their stagecraft and if you didn't see it then this live album will have to do. Some people can't chew gum and walk at the same time. Keith, Carl and Greg chewed gum while performing this stuff in concert. That's an impressive skill when you consider how complicated the musical arrangements were. I have read that this album wasn't a good representation of their live sound. I disagree because if you turn it up loud, it will push your face in and blow the roof off your dwelling. That you can see and feel.

Live Album Review

17-11-10

BY: ELTON JOHN

Before Sir Elton became Captain Fantastic, he was simply fantastic. The live album *17-11-10* was a heavily boot-legged radio broadcast that the record company released. "*Tumbleweed Connection*" (which I think is his finest work) was in the stores and this stripped down set featured some songs from that album.

'Stripped down' means it was Elton on piano and vocals, Nigel Olsson on drums and vocals, and Dee Murray on bass and vocals. That's it and all that's needed. The music jumps out at you from the first piano chord and Elton carries the show all by himself. And can that boy play! "*Take Me to the Pilot*" and "*Bad Side of the Moon*" are lesser known tunes of his, but in the early days, when he was up and coming, they were a showcase for his talents. "*Honky Tonk Women*" with its opening three-part harmony and piano driven honky-tonk, is the best interpretation of the song I have ever heard. It's probably how Keith Richards intended it to sound from the beginning.

The killer performance is the concluding medley of "*Burn Down the Mission*", "*My Baby Left Me*", and "*Get Back*". Reginald Dwight plays some majestic piano on "*Burn Down the Mission*" and the rhythm section holds it all together, allowing him to show off a little. This is quite a feat, if you're familiar with the studio version from Tumbleweed Connection.

Elton then segues into a jazzy improvisation that shows he could have had a credible career in that arena had he wanted to. It is obvious that he has a strong connection with his band. Nigel Olsson is an incredible drummer and Dee Murray plays unique bass patterns not found in his studio efforts. They follow him perfectly as he slides effortlessly into a brief rendition of the Elvis Presley song "*My Baby Left Me*". It's not over yet, because with energy to burn The Beatles' "*Get Back*" finishes it off, before Elton thanks the crowd of about a hundred people (so I'm told).

Elton John has said this was the best live recording he has ever done. I agree, and there is a legend that Elton John cut himself during the finale, resulting in blood covering the keyboards at the end of the show. Take that Slash. Take that Warren Zevon. Elton wasn't taking any prisoners during his early days and I sometimes wish he would have remained in that state of fury. That usually resulted in flaming out early

Live Album Review

and he was smart enough to not be a candle in the wind. A CD version that contains the complete 60 minute show is out there but I prefer the vinyl record. Go ahead, call me sentimental, but this is Elton John when he was truly mental. I liked the unpredictable kid, when he was in the closet and crazy. Then he had to get famous and become fashionably insane.

LIVE! RAISIN' HELL

BY: ELVIN BISHOP

"Alright, alright, alright!" That's Elvin Bishop addressing the crowd on this double live set *RAISIN' HELL* from 1977. Obviously the place was not filled to capacity but his southern charm and humor rose above it. The squares stayed home. This album is one of my favorite live sets by anybody. Elvin has a great band and even a young Mickey Thomas, who would later join Starship. The production values are pristine and the music is hot, classic Bishop, at his best.

"Sure Feels Good", *"Fooled Around And Fell In Love"*, *"Stealing Watermelons"*, *"Juke Joint Jump"*. Elvin's guitar is on fire and he's having a ball. He's just a 'good ol' boy' from Arkansas that made good. The song, *"Little Brown Bird"* is slow blues mastery and downright dirty. The killer is *"Traveling Shoes"*. That rendition never gets old and as one of his songs says, you wanna, 'jump, jump, jump' when you listen to it. The band rocks with alotta soul. Horns blaring, guitars bursting, vocalists singing with a holy ghost fervor. What

Live Album Review

more do you want ?

His lyric, from the song about getting a baseball bat to deal with his hard headed woman would get him arrested today. I wonder if he has changed it when he performs it now ? The concluding medley of "*Good Times Roll*", "*Change Is Gonna Come*", and "*Bring It On Home*" only makes the listener want more.

This is music that makes you feel good. The whole album gives off that vibe. When you listen to it you feel good. That's the real power of music in my opinion. Elvin Bishop is one of those musicians that can accomplish that feat.

LIVE!

BY: FOGHAT

LIVE! is Foghat in 1977 at their most popular. The band was born from Savoy Brown, where they learned their craft, developed their chops and moved on to steer their own ship by playing powerhouse blues. This live set was when Foghat was selling out stadiums. The songs are energized (pardon the pun) and delivered at maximum volume. The standards are here. *"I Just Want To Make Love To You"*, *"Fool For The City"* and *"Slow Ride"*. What Foghat show wouldn't be complete without them? It's the songs, *"Honey Hush"* with its *"Train Kept A Rollin' riff"* and *"Home In My Hand"* with its melodic chorus, that keep things interesting.

Lonesome Dave Peverett on guitar and lead vocals has perfected his craft. He doesn't have a great blues-type voice but can deliver the goods. Rod Price's slide work is wicked with his nasty tone and endless sustain. Yes, this single album is what you would expect from Foghat, but there really isn't a true concert experience here.

Live Album Review

They perform the songs much like the studio versions, only faster with little improvisation. No, it's just hard rock, boogie blues, sung and played by four guys, being true to who they are. They settled on a particular sound, got lucky with it, and didn't try to play outside the box. Overall, it's a good listen but rather skimpy because it clocks in at 38 minutes. It certainly makes you want to say, "Gimme More!"

Edward Milano

FRAMPTON COMES ALIVE!

BY: PETER FRAMPTON

What else can we say about *FRAMPTON COMES ALIVE!* that hasn't already been said? Maybe a different question should be asked. Why was it so popular? If you didn't have a copy, you knew someone that did. You listened to it, even if you didn't want to. It was everywhere. Maybe the answer is that it was good. In 1976, Peter Frampton was a struggling artist. His albums didn't sell well, and he was nothing more than an opening act or headlined at small venues. They hatched a good idea to release a live album of his excellent songs. I guess it worked. There are so many statistics out there about the sales I'm not even going to bother with, other than to put it in terms: "mo money, mo money."

From the opening, *"Something's Happening"* followed by the homage to The Doobie Brothers, *"Doobie Wah"*, the album is one wonderful song after another. The sound quality is exceptional, the band is tight and Peter's guitar playing is tasty. His vocals are average, but on-key and strong,

Live Album Review

and the pacing of the songs are perfect. The two opening numbers, followed by the hit single, "*Show Me The Way*", where Pete breaks out the talk-box, gets things moving. The semi-rocker of "*It's A Plain Shame*" leads into the mellow, let's snuggle by the fire, tunes of "*All I Want To Be*" (I never could figure out the lyric of "I don't care if they cut my hair"), "*Wind Of Change*", "*Baby I Love Your Way*", and "*I Wanna Go to the Sun*". Somebody made sure the girly screams from the audience are heard on this laid-back stuff. "*Penny for Your Thoughts*", I always thought, was a throw away instrumental, but it is nice and thankfully brief. Budding guitar players, at the time, learned to play it. It's more Paul McCartney than Steve Howe, but if you could play it at a party, you were a neat guy. Now the real rock is unearthed.

"*I'll Give You Money*" is reminiscent of his Humble Pie days. Yes, that clean-cut, nice boy was in that band of hedonists. He pays tribute by performing "*Shine On*" that launches into "*Jumpin' Jack Flash*". These three songs have some muscle and the band is hot and sweaty. Peter's lead guitar is fluid with some crunch. Take a breath for now the adult music is showcased. "*Lines on My Face*" is cool and expressive. It's a great lead up to the show-stopper, "*Do You Feel Like We Do?*" This song is a Peter Frampton, virtuoso, see and listen to what I can do, extravaganza. He literally makes his guitars speak. Okay, not funny, but he gives a shout-out to Bob Mayo, forever immortalizing him. I wish he would have said my name.

Edward Milano

Live Album Review

LIVE!

BY: GENESIS

This is a great live album. I remember seeing this in the stores in 1973 and wanted it. The only problem was I didn't have enough cash, not to mention I never heard of this band. The cover was enough to tell me what was inside was interesting. AM radio never played them, and the cool FM stations were too hip to give them airtime, and nobody I knew had any of their music. It wasn't till a couple years later when I saw it in a cut-out bin for a buck that I bought it and once I got it home and on the turntable; I was not disappointed.

Listening to it today, some 40 years later, it's as good as it was then. *"Watcher of The Skies"*, *"Get 'Em Out By Friday"*, *"The Knife"*, *"Return of The Giant Hogweed"*, and *"The Musical Box"*. The shortest song is over eight minutes long. These guys put the Art in Art Rock. No self indulgent, classical music passages that progressive rock of the day offered. This was a total band composition and everybody shined.

Live Album Review

Here's the band in 1973: Peter Gabriel on vocals, Steve Hackett on guitar, Michael Rutherford on guitar and bass, Tony Banks on Keys and some dude named Phil Collins on drums. This was music that was meant to be listened to. Sure, there was a theatrical element because of Peter Gabriel and the costumes he wore for each song. He took on the character of each song and I think over time, some of those characters became part of his psyche.

It's as if you're reading a novel when you listen to the lyrical content of each song. The stories are incredible and that's what they are: stories. The rest of the band was too busy concentrating on the complicated music to offer much of a stage presence, but who needs to? This is music you pay attention to. Who cares if the band doesn't jump around on the stage? Are the songs long? Sure, but boring? No way.

These live versions are better than the studio versions and the audience's reaction after each song ends is thunderous. Of course, later on, Genesis would become a huge band and Phil Collins would go on to be whatever it is he became. Peter Gabriel didn't do so bad and Mike And The Mechanics had a good run, as well as Steve Hackett, who's still vital today. Hey this was when these guys were a bunch of nobodies. To tell you the truth, I liked their music better before they all became somebody's.

SPACE RITUAL

BY: HAWKWIND

The noises and unsettling music that opens this live album is just a countdown, for as the muffled, transistorized voice speaks, it's blast off and for the next hour plus, you are on spacecraft, Hawkwind. Don't worry, the sonic attack of early BOC engulfs you with the controls set to the heart of Syd Barrett. Throw in some Motorhead for extra rocket fuel and add some vocal stylings from The Haight to keep the hippy vibe real.

SPACE RITUAL from 1973 was ahead of its time and probably was a miscalculation for release in a banner year for live albums. Hawkwind had to compete with the likes of Traffic, Uriah Heep, Ten Years After, Neil Young, Deep Purple, Genesis, Focus and Yes, who all dropped concert sets as well. I didn't have the cash to invest in all that, especially when *SPACE RITUAL* got no love from the critics and little to no promotion from the record company. Even if the double LP had amazing art and weirdness in the gatefold. It has

Live Album Review

aged well over time, due in part to Lemmy Kilmister but let's not kid ourselves, the music was too underground for mass appeal and hippies were passe.' It took a few decades for this to gain notoriety and now sits on various lists of great albums.

I don't know who compiles these lists, but to be considered one of the essential albums to hear before you die is kind of morbid. Hawkwind was touring in support of *DOREMI FASOL LATIDO* where the performances from *SPACE RITUAL* were pulled from gigs in Liverpool and London. England was their core audience and where their cosmic rock was accepted as an extension of the acid drenched 60s.

The return voyages from trips into the beyond brought back inspiration, with some help from Michael Moorcock's sci-fi mind. It was heavier than Elton's, Bowie's and Bolan's candy rock, space opera singles. "*Rocket Man*", "*Space Oddity*", and "*Ballrooms of Mars*" couldn't hang with Hawkwind's blitz. I'd take "*Silver Machine*" over that stuff any day, or forever.

I'd take the stage show as well. Too bad the audio doesn't provide that, for it was part of the deal. Excessive lights, video and Stacia doing her interpretive dancing with her heavenly body. There was no risk of hooliganism at a show because all the dudes in front had erections, so slam dancing could be injuriously painful. Tell us about the music. Okay, I will. It's non-stop, a 'Sonic Attack.' It's explained in detail, effectively narrated by Robert Calvert, who is credited for "*Poet and Swizzle*". He adds his talents to "*10 Seconds of Forever*" and "*7 By 7*". "*Space is Deep*" is deep. Things that make you lay awake at night in wonder. The spoken word essays are sandwiched between the blare.

"*Earth Calling*" is a good one but "*Orgone Accumulator*" is a better one. I didn't even know that contraption was a real thing. These rocks, as the majority of the show does, with a few, mellow glides on the celestial winds. "*Electronic No, 1*" is exactly what it says it is and everything fits to make for a great trip into the outer worlds. Melodic extended guitar or synth solos with a smattering of woodwinds. Dave Brock on vocals and guitar, Nik Turner on woodwinds, Dik Mik on electronics, Del Dettmar on synthesizer and Simon King on drums are the real thing and are all in with the vision. I'm not sure Lemmy was, which is why his exit papers were served, in his words, for "doing the wrong drugs." That turned out okay for Motorhead, taken from a Hawkwind song, was his calling.

If they moved next door and your grass would die, then Hawkwind moving next door would cause strange things to grow. 'Do not panic' we are instructed. Time We Left This World Today is an Awakening from the Master of

Live Album Review

the Universe who is having a Brainstorm while Upside Down. Please, don't panic. It will never make sense. Just go with it and remember, we were 'Born to Go.' I guess there's a story here, but why waste good energy and oxygen in trying to decipher the codes? It's Science Fiction and the possibilities are endless.

My understanding is that it's about the music of the spheres. YES traveled that way,at least Jon Anderson did on *OLIAS OF SUNHILLOW*, but comparing the two is like a lush forest and a burning desert. Rock and roll in the *"Black Corridor"*. It will be over before you know it. On the 10th second of forever you listened to *SPACE RITUAL*, is a welcome from the future where you are now a Space Lord. Lemmy didn't want to be a Space Lord, as it turns out. He was more comfortable being the Ace of Spades because he plays like Geezer Butler on Hawkwind songs.

It's a foregone conclusion that one would be apt to isolate Lemmy's work here with his sound in Motorhead. His passing only elevated Hawkwind to a more nostalgic status as that band he was once a member of. He takes a backseat on the shuttle with them. They were a sum of its parts, and that's what made the ship fly as far as it did. If you want to experience a genuine experience before you die, then this is the dilithium crystal for you. Morbid, I know. I have heard it on countless occasions and am still alive, so I know I got that goin' for me.

PERFORMANCE ROCKIN' THE FILLMORE

BY: HUMBLE PIE

This is the album that put Humble Pie on the map. Peter Frampton was still in the band and it's pretty evident that his contributions made them better. Recorded and released in 1971, *PERFORMANCE / ROCKIN' THE FILLMORE*, is Humble Pie staking their claim in the hard rock arena that they were a force to be reckoned with. From the opening salvo of *"Four Day Creep"*, where all three vocalists take turns singing a verse, it's more of an introduction by the band to the world that, "We have arrived. Now, what are you going to do about it?"

The energy is relentless. The riffs are edgy, the rhythm section is tight, and the interplay of Frampton's and Mariott's guitars is spectacular. It doesn't let up from there. This concert has it all, and it showcases the band's talents and good taste. The in your face rock that borders on heavy metal of *"Stone Cold Fever"*, and *"I'm Ready"*, the slow walking blues

Live Album Review

and guitar showmanship of "*I Walk On Gilded Splinters*", and the gut crunching guitar riffs with a soft porn scat singing of "*Rolling Stone*" that would make even Peter Wolf blush. There's even a harmonica solo in it, along with a call and response section with the audience. It's a rock song that includes everything, and none of it feels contrived. "*I Don't Need No Doctor*" is an FM classic and hearing it today is as fresh as it was in 1971.

Humble Pie was on fire that night. When they released this record, they were putting the Rolling Stones on notice that they were better and that they too walked a dangerous path and could deliver postcards from the edge just as horrifying. The Stones had managed to piss off The Hell's Angels, so who better than Humble Pie to blast in and fill the void? The Who would also have to recognize that The Pie were every bit as powerful on stage and didn't need any instrument smashing circus. Yes indeed, this was one of the pioneer albums designed for the car. Best listened to full blast, on the 8 Track, while copping a buzz.

Unfortunately, Peter Frampton decided to leave the band for mellower pastures, resulting in Humble Pie becoming The Steve Marriott Band (he has never been properly recognized). Future albums would contain a good tune or two, but they were nothing more than attempts to try, and recapture lightning in a bottle, which they never really did. So, if you don't have a Humble Pie album and want to have a Humble Pie album... this is the Humble Pie album to have.

RUNNING ON EMPTY

BY: JACKSON BROWNE

Jackson Browne made a career altering decision in 1977 to release music accessible to a larger audience. Being a sensitive singer / songwriter had a limited audience (mostly females). To get the Eagles crowd on board, he needed to toughen up some. *RUNNING ON EMPTY* is a road album, recorded on stage, in hotel rooms, backstage, and on the tour bus. It did the trick. It sold and was nominated for a couple of Grammys. To show you how lousy the music scene was at the time, he lost to Barry Manilow and the soundtrack to *SATURDAY NIGHT FEVER.* 'Enuff said'.

The song, *"Running On Empty"* is the lead song and Jackson Browne rocks. He never sounded so good. Thank David Lindley's slide guitar work. This album made David a household name and as it should have. The guy is brilliant. *"The Road"* is a number recorded in a hotel room. This approach is genius and Jackson took a page from the Zappa book of how to record albums on the cheap. You already

Live Album Review

have the musicians on the payroll, so use them. Skip the studio costs and time restrictions. Get everybody drunk and high and cut loose. "Rosie" is a throwback to Jackson's romantic, sweet stuff the ladies love him for. "You Love The Thunder" rocks like pre-Joe Walsh Eagles. "Cocaine" is another hotel room recording, and the fiddle makes the slow crawl of the song work. Otherwise, it's a weary tune. "Shakey Town" borrows from "The Weight" but that's an excellent song to steal from, so Jackson gets a pass. "Love Needs A Heart" is the chick magnet doing what he does best. "Nothing But Time" is a tour bus recording and you can hear the engines during the tune, which is kind of funny.

"The Load Out/Stay" is the song that perfectly bookends this album with the title track. Despite being overplayed on the radio, this song still sounds fresh today. David Lindley's falsetto is always cool to hear and the song's message seems sincere. The basic theme of the endless road struggles of touring meets the listener with a message that the show is the payoff (as well as a payday).

It continues to be appreciated as an effective tribute by the audience. I don't think Jackson Browne was able to capture lightning in a bottle again after this release. He had some hits and decent albums, but nothing close to this classic. Maybe his environmental and political activism killed his creativity. I will say David Lindley and El-Rayo X made three excellent albums after this.

MAD DOGS AND ENGLISHMEN

BY: JOE CROCKER

In 1970, Joe Cocker was a hot commodity. His first two albums were hits and his performance at Woodstock in 1969 was the stuff of legend. He was a young star, in need of some rest and relaxation, but management forced him to stay on the road, with the alleged threat of bodily harm.

Leon Russell is the musical visionary here, and his fingerprints and trademark sound is all over this. Leon Russell, who produced Joe Cocker's second album, agreed to put together a band for an American tour, with total control, replacing Joe's capable Grease Band that had previously backed him in the studio and on the road. There's a seemingly cast of thousands. Besides Leon, there's Jim Keltner, Don Preston, Chris Stainton (who was Joe's best friend and musical cohort), Bobby Keyes, Billy Preston, Carl Radle, Jim Gordon, Rita Coolidge... I could go on but I won't.

What's surprising is there's no stellar guitar work on this. Leon plays the guitar. It's almost as if he decided to keep

Live Album Review

it heavy on rhythm and keyboards. There are two drummers, two percussionists, two keyboard players and horns aplenty, but this is 1970 and Jimmy Page played that great guitar riff on the studio version of *"A Little Help From My Friends"*. Can we have some killer guitar? I'm not sure who financed this tour and movie, but I'm sure they sold it in the boardrooms to a group of investors that rock and roll movies make money, especially if the soundtrack sells. They put a lot into the double album packaging, that's for sure. I'm not sure how much of the liner notes is true, but it's an entertaining read.

Anyway, the music contained here is classic Cocker: *"Delta Lady"*, *"The Letter"*, *"Cry Me a River"*, *"She Came in Through the Bathroom Window"*. His signature song, *"A Little Help from My Friends"* is omitted, but maybe one Beatle song is enough. The Stones, Dylan, Traffic and Joe were able to tap into the cool contemporary music of the day, but do it differently than a typical cover band playing local bars. He had a voice and style that turned every tune into his own unique creation. There's a blues set featured on this set and is where Joe shines the brightest. *"Superstar"* making the cut is curious, primarily because one lady in the choir sings it and because some excellent songs from the concert were left off the album.

Hey, Leon wrote it and needs some royalty money too if not the spotlight. It is clear this whole circus was the Leon Russell Show and Joe Cocker was one of the performers, even if his name is on the marquee. To stay relevant, they have to toss in a topical song, *"Give Peace A Chance"*. This is actually a Leon Russell composition and way different from John Lennon.

Hosting some incredible shows, The Fillmore East sure did deliver, and this one ranks right up there. The band is excellent, but they should be considering who's in it. The choir is great and at the conclusion of *"Delta Lady"* they are singing with such emotion, it's apparent this was a once -in-a -lifetime experience. Joe says to the crowd, as the song is winding down, "rock and roll." Is that what you call it? I don't hear much of that on this. The opener, *"Honky Tonk Women"* is the closest this band gets to rock and roll. I would call it 'corporate rock.' This whole thing was drawn-up and designed in an office somewhere. That doesn't make it bad. In fact, it's better than good. One of the very few times the suits actually got it right. What they got wrong was the toll it took on the star attraction.

The tour would end after this performance and this commune, of sorts, would go their separate ways. Joe never scaled the heights he did here again. He was burnt-out and fried from the pace, the pressure, and amount of drugs and booze he consumed. People have remarked later that he was never the same after this tour. It looked as though the rock machine had eaten another one of its young, sacrificed

Live Album Review

on the altar of greed. He came away from this penniless and crashing on a friend's couch. Sure, he later had some good songs and a long career, but *MAD DOG AND ENGLISHMEN* is like winning the Super Bowl in your rookie season and then never making the playoffs again.

Edward Milano

Live Album Review

YOU CAN'T ARGUE WITH A SICK MIND

BY: JOE WALSH

You can't argue with a sick mind. Good advice and it happens to be the title of Joe Walsh's live album from 1976. He would join The Eagles soon after. If that was a good thing or a bad thing is another matter. What's good is this record. It's perfect.

"*Walk Away*" opens the set, and it's a unique arrangement from The James Gang version. You can feel his band is tight, locked in and enjoy the music they are playing. I guess they would be too considering who his backing band was: Don Felder on guitar, Joe Vitale and Andy Newmark on drums, Willie Weeks on bass, Jay Ferguson and David Mason on keyboards and someone named Rocky Dzidzoru on percussion.

On "*Meadows*" they stretch the song into a tasteful, all-purpose jam. "*Rocky Mountain Way*" has Joe and Don Felder trading guitar licks during the solo, and Joe's talk-box work is more interesting than 'he who will not be named.'

"*Help Me Through the Night*" is like the eye of the hurricane. Acoustic and mellow, it even features guest vocals from Don Henley, Glenn Frey in addition to Don Felder. It's an excellent performance to say the least. The killer here is "*Turn to Stone*". It begins quietly with the keyboards inter-playing a beautiful, new age-y arrangement before Joe's monster power chords come blasting in. After presenting the actual song, the band takes it into jazz territory and brings out the flutes. Why? Who knows, but it works. The whole album works. In fact, this album could almost be the forerunner for what the jam bands today are doing. If you enjoy that genre of music, then you'll really enjoy this. If not, I'll guarantee you'll enjoy this, anyway, good music is good music.

Live Album Review

AT SAN QUENTIN

BY: JOHNNY CASH

1969 was a good year for Johnny Cash. He was just another country artist till this release. The San Quentin album followed up The Folsom Prison set that did well. This one crossed him over. He won numerous awards for this, one including the Grammy for Album of the Year. All really on the strength of a Shel Silverstein song, *"Boy Named Sue"*. I still think it is the first *"Gangsta Rap"* song.

The full concert was re-released later, which of course, included a ton of material, but I like the original just as it is. It starts with *"Wanted Man"*, a song he co- wrote with Bob Dylan, and ends with the short, 'chunka,chunka' of *"Folsom Prison Blues"*. The album has 10 songs, with spurts of audience interaction, and it is more than enough. Listening to this, you realize Johnny Cash was authentic. I believe that's why he could crossover into the musical territories occupied by the anti-establishment. Outlaw Country was at its genesis here, and Johnny Cash helped pave the way. Dylan endorsing him didn't hurt, but it's the fact that he was honest, admitted he wrestled with demons in his personal life and walked a hard road. Redemption and salvation were something he was never shy about sharing. He had a real heart for those in places of bondage, both physical, and behind the walls of a prison. He knew that he could have ended up in jail or dead himself. Most people of his generation said, "Do as I say, not as I do." His legend grew as time went on, that echoes today, after he has passed. Here is an impressive document of 'The Man in Black' playing to a captive audience.

Live Album Review

KISS ALIVE!

BY: KISS

Is this a real live album? *KISS ALIVE!* released in 1975, and to be honest, they were on the verge of fading away into obscurity. Their record label was all but bankrupt, and although the band was generating a solid fan base from touring, record sales were less than desirable. They were broke. I know this because I was a fan and bought their first three albums. Most people thought they were Alice Cooper clones. I happened to think their music was pretty good (then).

This album, from the back cover, would make you think the show was recorded in Detroit. The album includes recordings from shows in Detroit, Ohio, New Jersey, and Iowa. Soldiers in the Kiss Army already know this stuff anyway. I didn't volunteer, or better yet, pay my dues to be in the ranks. After *DESTROYER*, the band was destroyed, as far as I was concerned.

Anyway, back to *KISS ALIVE*. Supposedly, the only real live music is the drum tracks. That's not important? This album broke the band into the big time and that was the goal. Great songs from the first three albums are here and some are still in rotation today: *"Deuce"*, *"Strutter"*, *"Firehouse"*, *"Black Diamond"*, *"Rock And Roll All Night"* and *"Hotter than Hell"*. They have as many catchy and meaningless songs as AC/DC and deliver them faster and louder.

The original band is here: Gene, Paul, Ace and Peter. The only stand out moments are Paul's guitar intro to *"Black Diamond"*, and Peter's drum solo on *"100,000 Years"*, *"Cold Gin"* is the best song. Paul's speech to set it up is classically stupid, but so what? They're not playing to rocket scientists here. I know you have heard it and many have it. It has personal memories for you, as well as me. Hey, I bought the album when it first came out and so did many others I went to High School with. I could only say, "See, I told ya so." Of course, with the album, we didn't get to witness the Freddie Krueger's of Rock with the blood spitting, fire breathing, fireworks, guitars on fire (all things pimple faced, long-haired High School dudes think is cool)...

MTV was still a few years away. No, we had to wait for the circus to come to town. There's a sucker born every minute, but when you know you're a sucker and choose to be one, then it's okay.

Live Album Review

THE SONG REMAINS THE SAME

BY: LED ZEPPELIN

THE SONG REMAINS THE SAME is the only live album Led Zeppelin would release during their active years. Taken from performances at Madison Square Garden in 1973, the album wasn't released until 1976. Jimmy Page didn't like it and considered it nothing more than a soundtrack to the movie of the same name. Maybe the soundtrack to one of the longest music videos is more accurate. That is a subject better discussed elsewhere, for this is about the album that has aged well. It sounds better today than it did when it originally dropped. By now, everyone has seen the movie and realized that the soundtrack album left off many songs from it. That had more to do with economics, for it would have been a triple album, which, by nature, cost more and sold less.

This is one of those albums that a person, in 1976, had the opportunity to hear, in different places, on different formats: in a bedroom on a record player, in a car through an 8-track player, on a cassette player or, if somebody was really cool, on a reel-to-reel. VHS wasn't available yet, so most people didn't see the movie anyway and before the days of cable, it wasn't going to be broadcast on television anytime soon. Depending on if the sound system was great, which was few and far between, the only common denominator is that you were listening to it buzzed.

Who really knew what was and what is? *THE SONG REMAINS THE SAME* is a live album, by a band that was huge and I mean Godzilla huge. From the opener of *"Rock and Roll"* to the closer of, *"Whole Lotta Love"*, fans and non-fans alike got to hear Led Zeppelin in concert, which was a different but excellent demonstration of their talent and showmanship. It also sounded great when you were 'high' which was 'the' true test.

I never saw the band live but kept reading about the hedonistic excesses, the occult influences and the endless party on the road. It seemed the press was more interested in reporting that side of the band than the music itself. The movie showed little to none of that and concentrated on the band playing their music. I saw the flick in the theaters and, other than the individual dream sequences, it was a great concert experience. I wanted to hear the album and felt disappointed when they left off some great songs. Okay, at least *"Stairway to Heaven"* is there and with Jimmy's creative additions to the introduction, it became a debate if this ver-

Live Album Review

sion was better than the studio one.

You know every punk that learned to play that intro on guitar had to learn those additional licks. It really came down to the fact that the live version was more engaging because we all heard the studio version a million times and were getting bored with it. To this day I don't know what Robert Plant means when he introduces the song as, "a song about hope." What's with, "does anybody remember laughter?" I didn't forget it and if this a dig at the Mr. Crowley crowd, I do know the band is some kind of good and considering it's all being done as a three-piece. It makes the performance even more incredible. There's Jimmy Page and his Gibson, double neck SG, John Paul Jones providing the flute/recorder, through keyboard simulation and quickly switching to bass duties, Bonzo keeping a steady but thunderous backbeat and Robert Plant's singing/screaming, loud and proud. He even adds some extras for the people who know every line, melody and turn, to identify the differences with a discerning ear. Why did Pagey dislike this stuff? If he wanted us to have an accurate representation of a Led Zep show, then why didn't he release one? This could and should have been improved, and the people had higher expectations, but they were only presented with this. Smoke 'em if ya got 'em.

Pagey made certain *"Dazed and Confused"* is included, all 27 minutes of it. Yeah, he bows his Les Paul during his solo spot but he's getting lost in the haze, without the stunning and colorful visuals, it takes some sheer will-power, by the listener, to get through the complete performance. He did look cool in the movie, with his hair a wet mess, as he sweated through the extended guitar break. Do you know how heavy a Les Paul is? That guy looked to be 100 pounds, soaking wet. How did he do it for over two hours? A little help from his friends? An acoustic set, sitting down would've helped. Wait, they had that in their show. They just don't have it here. There's still an impressive rendition of *"The Song Remains the Same"* that transitions the band from heavy duty, English blues-based rockers to pompous, gentlemen of prog-rock.

It's stuff like this that makes this live album/ soundtrack so much better than the critics gave it credit for being. People were so familiar with the studio songs that the live versions showed a different band with a different approach. John Paul Jones' haunting keyboards on *"No Quarter"* and Page delivering the crunch is a good example. John Bonham's drum solo on *"Moby Dick"* is a chance to understand, as well as have a document of his powerful sensitivity to give you the ammunition to argue his skills over Ian Paice or Keith Moon.

Wonderful stuff on this album. I know Page released an expanded version, as well as archived concerts, decades

Live Album Review

later, but this was the first, and in my opinion, the best one, because it was when the band was still a functioning unit. When it came out, the band had already released *PHYSICAL GRAFFITI* and *PRESENCE*. Things were changing, and the lifestyle was catching up to them. The devil was due and their soft targets were vulnerable. *THE SONG REMAINS THE SAME* was when they were at their best and nobody knew, at the time, how the story would play out. We were just happy to get what they gave us. You knew it was going to be good.

LEON LIVE!

BY: LEON RUSSEL

LEON LIVE! The title says all that needs saying. His first name along with the picture on the front cover is an announcement more than a clever marketing scheme. People in the early seventies were aware of him because of *JOE COCKER MAD DOGS AND ENGLISHMEN* in 1970. Who could forget his presence and contributions to *THE CONCERT FOR BANGLADESH* in 1972?

Not many were hip to his session work but that information is not important. What is important is that *LEON LIVE*, from 1973, is the album that finally let everyone in on what those in the music industry were keeping on the down-low. After all, only two things come out of Oklahoma.

Stepping out of the confines of the studio, Leon Russell put together a traveling roadshow, almost identical to the one he did for Joe Cocker. Remember Leon's performance in the Bangladesh charity show? George Harrison was wise to enlist his talents for it would have been a different show

Live Album Review

and probably a sloppier one if Leon wasn't involved.

This album, *LEON LIVE!* is from two concerts in Long Beach, California in 1972. It was originally a three record set (not to be outdone by some of his contemporaries) that almost seemed to be the norm in those days and I'm perplexed it sold as well as it did for who had that kind of cash? Three records are more of a metaphor for Leon's show, as well as his creative output at this point in his career. Simply stated, it's over abundance with extreme excellence.

This set contains so much information that one could write a book about it. I could try but will probably fall short, but that's okay for the rock, and roll boogie gospel rhythm and blues gumbo is a reward all by itself and ya'll know, everyone listens differently anyway.

"*Mighty Quinn Medley: I'll Take You There and Idol With the Golden Head*" is the 12 minute opening and is a show all in itself. Leon Russell leads his people and I say people, for he's the master of ceremonies and his musicians and vocalists are an extension of himself. Heck, he could probably play all the instruments as well, if not better than his band, but he only has two hands and one mouth, so he has to delegate the grandeur in his head to others. He trusts them, that's for sure. Joey Cooper and Don Preston on guitars, Carl Radle on bass, Rev. Patrick Henderson on keys, Chris Blackwell on drums, Ambrose Campbell on percussion and five, count 'em five, back-up vocalists, all sing and play with love and abandon. This is a show where the musicians and singers are giving their all and leaving it on the stage. At no time during the 19 songs is there a time-out or a haphazard performance. It cooks from the get-go and doesn't stall once. Leon's "southern drawl'" may influence this writing a little, and he does come off as an Okie when he talks (or preaches) to the audience. I am perplexed by this and am sure he wasn't ashamed of his roots, but this man was a genius. His brilliance shines through the music, but still he chose to maintain the persona of a tribal leader with an 'aw-shucks' attitude. He didn't call himself "The Master of Time and Space" for no reason. This guy had an eccentric personality, but he remained grounded enough to create some amazing music. I wonder if he could get away with his tribute to Little Richard *Crystal Closet Queen*" today and does anyone else think his version of *"Delta Lady"* trumps Joe Cocker's?

Anyway, after listening to the opening introduction, I always felt that the album cover should have had a disclaimer stamped on it. Do you remember those albums that said, 'Play Loud?', well this one should say, 'Play In A Tent', for this is an old-time gospel hour and Brother Love's Traveling Salvation tour. This is a rock and roll church and Leon lets everyone know there's power and love in the music. Dylan would be impressed by using this sound on his 'Saved' tour. Speaking of Zimmy, more than one of his songs are featured here,

Live Album Review

reworked of course, but there's an unspoken connection that goes beyond just a loving tribute. Maybe it was a message to Bob to persuade him to get back in the game.

After close to two hours of being absorbed by this album, I can honestly say it's a memory that needed rediscovering, just as Leon Russell's music career needs rediscovering. You can hear his influence on artists like Billy Joel from the piano work on "*Queen of the Roller Derby*", to Ian Hunter on the song, "*Roll Away The Stone*".

Mott the Hoople did a song of the same name but the piano work on the Leon tune reminds one of the pounding ivories on "*All The Way From Memphis*". The song, "*Prince of Peace*" has a melody that Gordon Lightfoot would borrow later and "*Stranger in a Strange Land*" could be the template for Jimmy Buffett. I do enjoy listening to Leon as he's translating the words to the 'Zulu' out -chorus of "*Out in the Woods*". He is speaking to the crowd but also to you, the individual. Yes, I do think the lyrics are beautiful and his explanation is kinda deep and Leon was part philosopher as well as musician and songwriter.

"*Jumpin' Jack Flash/Young Blood*" is like the version he did for the Bangladesh album, but it's ten minutes longer. The song is significantly better because he doesn't have to contend with an army of under-rehearsed musicians. Yes lawd and amen, that band is him. He chose his back-up commune well and his production has them playing up, down and all around. If you're familiar with Spector's Wall of Sound, then Leon takes it further to where the music is an Ocean of Sound. You have to listen to all of it and if you do, then it surrounds you. The vocalists, the pianos, the guitars, the drums and percussion all have an interpersonal language amongst themselves and they weave a musical tapestry that is good for the soul, or as Leon describes it, "The Power of Music." I get it now, Leon, and thank you.

Live Album Review

WAITING FOR COLUMBUS

BY: LITTLE FEAT

This album is a classic with a capital 'C'! If you have little to no knowledge of the band Little Feat, then 1978's *WAITING FOR COLUMBUS* would be an excellent crash course. Jam bands today all took a page from the Little Feat book of 'How to Play a Great Concert to a Crowd of High People'. This is a double album of greatness. There's not one terrible song in the set. This audio is taken from performances in 1977 at London's Rainbow Theatre, and The Risner in Washington D.C.

"Fat Man in the Bathtub" is one of the greatest songs ever in the rock era, and it even has a cowbell!To start the show with that song sets the bar high. Listing all the tunes is a waste of time. The best of Little Feat's best is here and the sound quality is excellent on *"Dixie Chicken"*, *"Oh Atlanta"*, *"Time Loves A Hero"*, *"Mercenary Territory"* and *"Sailin' Shoes"*.

I'll stop now. I won't say that *"Willin"* is the best truck driving song in history. I won't say *"Don't Bogart That Joint"* is forever imprinted on the brains of anyone who ever smoked dope with friends. Not to mention Jimmy Buffett, who hijacked the idea, and wrote his own goofy song for the audience to join in with *"Why Don't We Get Drunk And Screw?"*. I Also won't mention The Tower of Power Horns or mention Lowell George is at the top of his talents, even if the historians say he was in decline.

Let's also give a shout-out to Bill Payne, Ritchie Hayward and Paul Barrere, who are all notable members of the family. Why Elliot Engbar gets a credit, I don't know. I think he was a pal of Lowell's during his brief involvement with Frank Zappa. Mick Taylor also gets a credit, but that's because he makes a guest appearance to play some dirty sounding slide guitar on *"A Apolitical Blues"*. Some of everybody shines as they stretch the songs out with groovy, funky fun and jams aplenty.

If this is your choice of bud, then this will get you there quicker because this album is Little Feat's finest moment and also their best seller. The original intention was for it to be a triple album, and they omitted three tracks: *"Red Streamliner"*, *"Teenage Nervous Breakdown"*, and *"Skin It Back"*. People can hear these tracks on the hodgepodge of *HOY HOY* from 1981, which was released after Lowell George passed away.

Live Album Review

A picture from the inside of the LP is from a sign at a concert venue where the band had played. It states: "No Admission to Anyone Wearing Motorbike Gear or Studded Clothing." It's too bad they didn't play Altamont. Then nobody would have gotten killed there.

Edward Milano

Live Album Review

LIVE! DEAD

BY: THE GRATEFUL DEAD

LIVE! DEAD, from 1969, is 'Ground Zero' for the jam band improvisational rock that followed in its wake. The Grateful Dead were not paying dividends for Warner Brothers, who had heavily invested into breaking them into a wider audience. Trying to capture the magic in the studio was restrictive and did not translate to middle America.

The Dead had an audience, and the music was made for their people, who were encouraged to 'tune in' so the band could take them further. "You have to be high to listen to it," isn't necessarily the case here for this double, live album lovingly features The Dead's live performance. They brought it from the stage and into the living room. They used 16 track recordings to allow the instruments and voices to be heard clearly. The sound is pristine, far removed from bootleg quality, but black lights, incense and recreational stimulants were the responsibility of the listener. The gang of Jerry, Bob, Phil, Bill and Micky are here. Tom Constanten provides the organ, and Pigpen is around. He's limited to vocals and organ on one song, and plays congas on everything else, but he's here and is a part of the family.

The album was a labor of intense dedication, from the album graphics that cleverly mask the word ACID, to the sequencing of the songs to provide a continuous ebb and flow. The outcome was successful. It received critical praise. It sold and sewed the seeds that grew the fan base from a cult into a community. The unorganized, loose band of hippies grew into a unified group of 'Dead Heads' with their own culture and language. "*Dark Star*" opens the show and after six minutes of noodling The Dead find the groove to enter the song. This song/jam/improvisational method lasts for twenty-three minutes. There is no interruption on the voyage where the band isn't able to return. They are all on the same astral plane. Interplay is working from the two drummers, who can play in unison or play off each other, while one locks in with Phil's outstanding bass runs, the other can play with expression. The guitars of Bob's rhythm and Jerry's lead are the real, ancient art of weaving that Keef was always trying to find in The Stones. The vocals are 'Dead' vocals. No powerful, distinct singing as much as a welcoming, non-threatening approach to communicate the lyrical tapestries. The complete performance takes up the complete Side 1 of the vinyl, which is by design. "*St. Stephen/Eleven*" is the whole of Side 2. It's performed to be a continuous wave of music. The band

Live Album Review

takes the audience on an almost brilliant jazz fusion groove after sharing the tale of St. Stephen. Moments like this happen when nobody has the tapes rolling and have to be described by spoken word essays. This moment captured why The Dead made history with their live shows. High or not, this is a great sixteen minutes of musical time that works in whatever state your personal head is in.

"*Turn on Your Love Light*" has rhythm and blues flavors, allowing the Dead's versatility of styles to be featured. The band jam on this as well and for 15 minutes, nothing has changed in the approach, other than the backbeat and the different road they are traveling. "*Death Don't Have No Mercy*" is where Pigpen gets to do the stuff he wants to do. He was a founding member and instead of focusing on blues-based material, The Grateful Dead ventured into psychedelia. Ron McKernan preferred liquor over LSD and wasn't all-in with the direction of the band. They gave him the opportunity to sing and play organ on a song that has become a Dead standard. This one is played almost straight, because the jam aspects pop up in a section titled "*Feedback*". Neil Young in his *WELD* period and Lou Reed's *METAL MACHINE MUSIC* has got nothing on this. It feels like the band is purposely making the beautiful trip of the audience into a real bummer. That's not very cool but after the harsh crash is over, the guys harmonize on a soft, "*We Bid You Goodnight*".

Edward Milano

Why did you guys do that? Was the feedback portion necessary? They included it on the album, in that specific spot, so an affirmative is the obvious answer; "Because we can!" isn't always the best reason to do something, but it's The Grateful Dead, and are free to do what they want. They signed a recording contract with that agreement. Their way of doing things is what made them a part of American history and culture. It's better not to question, but to trust they always had our best interests at heart.

Live Album Review

ROCK AND ROLL ANIMAL

BY: LOE REED

ROCK AND ROLL ANIMAL from 1974 is Lou Reed's transformation from his album *BERLIN* to David Bowie land. In fact, if you listen carefully, you can hear David Bowie all over this set. Makes sense, considering David Bowie hijacked Lou Reed's approach and put his own stamp on it, making millions while Lou Reed suffered with heroin addiction.

This live album was a mind blower. Lou Reed never sounded so good. He actually rocks and his voice actually carries a semblance of a tune. Well, the rocking is courtesy of guitarists Dick Wagner and Steve Hunter. You might as well call this a Wagner/Hunter album, and Lou Reed just sings on it.

The introduction to *"Sweet Jane"* is nothing short of brilliance. Just that introduction alone makes this whole album worth getting. *"White Light/White Heat"* sounds like vintage David Bowie And The Spiders From Mars.

"*Rock and Roll*" the two guitarists flexing their muscles for ten minutes. This album was a career boost for Reed. Too bad Hunter and Wagner didn't stick around. Lou Reed's work in the 70s, since this record, was uneven and even at times bizarre. They ended up working with Alice Cooper when he went solo and their work on the albums *WELCOME TO MY NIGHTMARE* and *GO TO HELL* are telling. Getting back to the intro to Sweet Jane. Call me crazy, but somehow I get the impression it inspired Johnny Cougar for his introduction to "*I Need A Lover*".

Live Album Review

ONE MORE FROM THE ROAD

BY: LYNYRD SKYNYRD

This album, *ONE MORE FROM THE ROAD*, by Lynyrd Skynyrd is the mountain. In 1976, when it was released they were poised to take their place alongside the heavyweights of The Stones, Led Zep and The Who. They probably would have surpassed them in legacy and greatness, but alas... tragedy. This band was snake-bit, cursed. Maybe the cover they do of *"Crossroads"* is a clue. All the familiar songs, now part of our culture, are here: *"Sweet Home Alabama"*, *"Tuesday's Gone"* and *"Free Bird"* It's a great double album by a band that apologized to no one.

These guys were a genuine family of wandering gypsies and Ronnie Van Zandt sat in the front wagon. Before: It was common knowledge that they were true, wild-eyed southern boys. They didn't need to name albums or write songs about it. They just were. Ronnie kept everyone in line because he probably could kick everyone's ass, one-at-a-time or collectively. On stage, he just stood there, barefooted, and sang but commanded attention, regardless. He had that powerful presence. His lyrics were deep water from a calm surface. He was an old soul- wise and full of simple man, common sense.

When he died, the soul of that band died and I think a part of America died too. The original Lynyrd Skynyrd represented the values of hard work, respect for elders, self-reliance, the right to defend yourself and your family and reverence to "The Man Upstairs." Scores of southern bands tried to follow in the wake, but it was nothing more than a facsimile formula. I think if Ronnie Van Zandt were alive today, he wouldn't be making music. I think he would be running for POTUS. I ain't joshing.

Live Album Review

KICK OUT THE JAMS

BY: MC5

"Good morning class. Please turn to page MC5 in your history book. Sid, would you please read aloud? I forgot, you can't read. Nancy, you may begin."

Instead of attending class and learning from a book, I elect to listen to this debut live album from the MC5 that was released in 1969 from two shows in 1968, at Detroit's Grande Ballroom. The infamous dates of these shows are October 30th and 31st. For those familiar with what traditionally occurs in the Detroit area on October 30th, or 'Devil's Night' this is the perfect band to play the soundtrack to the carnage. They were present in August of that year at the Democratic National Convention in Chicago and it's well documented what happened on the streets during this event. Who better than the MC5 to represent the voice of the youth and incite them to action? It was a turbulent time in America, no doubt about it. It would take too much space to analyze it and how this band of garage rockers rose to such a revered place in the history books.

When the album was originally dropped, Rolling Stone magazine hated it. Today, they include it in the list of top 500 albums of all time. It's funny how "time wounds all heels," as John Lennon once said. He got caught up in all that 'revolution stuff' for a time but later confessed to his being manipulated by Abbie Hoffman and Jerry Rubin. It is clear that John Sinclair had the same intent with his management of the MC5, when he admitted that the band wanted to be bigger than The Beatles.

White Panther Party and Yippies aside, it can all be debated, discussed and derailed for hours. Let's just decide to leave that portal into the counterculture past and embrace the world of the now. Drop the needle into grooves and listen to Sinclair as he preaches revolution from the stage with buzz words and phrases, getting the crowd worked up before MC5 hits the stage. The opening salvo of "*Ramblin' Rose*" has Wayne Kramer singing, and he sounds like Tiny Tim backed by a sloppier version of Blue Cheer. Why? I don't know, but the crowd doesn't seem to mind.

Without so much as a pause, they kick it with "*Kick Out the Jams*" complete with the classic expletive introduction. Which was and remains the template for future punks, garage bands, and even metal heads. I think it's the introduction and the brass of the record company to release it uned-

Live Album Review

ited, that is the real hook. The song itself was never a great tune to begin with, but the energy and the aggression from the MC5 inspired many to grab a guitar or sticks and pound out their own ethos. The phrase "kick out the jams" was hijacked by Sinclair and used as a call to revolution, but the band wrote it as a message to the hippie bands and blues-based Brits to refrain from jamming so much on stage and get down to the business of playing music.

This album is sequenced to be a relentless assault. *"Come Together"*, *"Rocket Reducer"*, and *"Borderline"* are all a mix of the Troggs' *"Wild Thing"*, and The Who's *"I Can See For Miles"* played faster, angrier, and at maximum, distorted volume. Wayne Kramer and Fred "Sonic" Smith are the fore-runners of the punk guitar methodology---play reasonably tight and make a lot of noise. If Paul McCartney tried to out loud The Who with *"Helter Skelter"*, then the MC5 took it it to the next level. They have said they were punk before punk, metal before metal, and MC before Hammer. They even had a minister of information, decades before Public Enemy. All is true, and man, this album is a testament to that. I still think of all the Michigan based bands from that era. Grand Funk Railroad did this stuff much better, but they aren't even an afterthought to the smart people that run the Rock and Roll Hall of Fame.

"Motor City Is Burning" is a twelve-bar blues exercise

and the only song from this set that is even close to having a real structure. Rob Tyner does his best white boy blues vocal over a heavier than a heavy progression of pounding on an anvil. The rhythm section of Michael Davis on bass and Dennis Thompson on drums can actually be heard, and they are solid musicians in their own right. When not having to provide the foundation of simplicity to anchor the war machine that sounds similar to early Black Sabbath. It sounds as if Ozzy was playing drums, Tony was on bass, Geezer played guitar, and Bill sang lead vocals.

It's pretty clear the frazzled and harsh sound is anything but carefully executed. The finale of "*Starship*" an eight-minute tune based on a piece by Son Ra, has been described as a "weird-out," and who am I to argue? The band has said the wash of psychedelia, lyrics about leaving this planet for a better one (I reckon that was the solution Sinclair was espousing from the stage), and the feedback, noodles, and burps were influenced by Ornette Coleman. That in itself tells you there was more under the surface of the MC5 than they were allowed or even felt confident enough to put on display. If they're pioneers, then it was by accident, but what a glorious wreck. Black Sabbath would borrow this theme for "*Into The Void*" and I'm sure Spock, with his Vulcan lute, jamming with the space hippies, was somewhere in the galaxy listening. "I'm going to Eden, yeah brother." So much for "kicking out the jams."

Live Album Review

Was this whole thing hype? I think so, but what do I know? I can just imagine the management trying to sell this band and persuade the record company to release this album amidst such civil unrest of the time. Nonetheless, you can't take anything away from this live set and the place it holds in rock music history. "One, two, three, what are we fighting for?" Country Joe would make that statement later, but kind of came off as a smart-ass you wanted to punch. I betcha Arlo Guthrie was smiling in a booth at Alice's restaurant. His take in 1967 was basically a comedy routine. It's all related and intertwined in the fabric of America today, but "Kick out the jams, Motherf***ers!" is the best and most honest slogan that still endures. I liken this album to a temper tantrum by young men, protesting a war they had no say in and not wanting to be drafted after seeing many of their kind come back in coffins. When a young person has a temper tantrum they can do a couple things. Run away (like many did to Canada), or yell curses, scream, and maybe break some things. This album is the latter, and it's a perfect representation of what was happening in 1968, but for my money The Who's Live at Leeds was better and more powerful, Hendrix playing *"The Star-Spangled Banner"* at Woodstock was more meaningful, and The Stones at Altamont were more dangerous. The rub is that all these events came after this.

LIVE!

BY: MOTT HOPPLE

This album was released at the end of Mott the Hoople. Mick Ralphs and Verden Allen had already left the fold and Ian Hunter tried to carry the torch but ended up having a nervous breakdown. Side one is from their eventful performance at The Odeon Theatre on Broadway and the band sounds tired. Side two is from a show at London's Hammersmith Theatre and Ian Hunter and the boys are in good spirits. The concluding, 16 minute medley of *"Jerkin Crocus/One of the Boys/Rock'n'Roll Queen/Get Back/Whole Lotta Shakin Goin' On/Violence"* is the best feature on the whole album.

One not versed in MTH history can get an idea of the power this band had, even with Ariel Bender and Morgan Fisher. *"Sweet Angeline"* has its moments and you get a good sense of Ian Hunter's showmanship. Historical footnote to side one is that the band Queen (remember them?) opened for Mott the Hoople on this particular tour in 1974. The song *"Marionette"* which can only be found on the ex-

Live Album Review

panded release, was the inspiration for Freddie Mercury to write *"Bohemian Rhapsody"*. One would need to hear the studio version on the album THE HOOPLE to get the full effect of the song. Besides Queen, scores of later musicians from England would cite Mott the Hoople as an influence, Mick Jones from The Clash and Joe Elliott of Def Leppard being just two of many. To really get an idea of Mott the Hoople, check out a live performance of *"Keep a Knockin"* from their 1971 album, *WILDLIFE*. In fact, check out the whole album. While you're at it, check out their album *MOTT*, which is one of the best albums by anyone, ever.

This is about live music here. I would only say this album is a document more than a must have. The band Mott the Hoople were basically a spent force when it was released, so it's more of a eulogy. Maybe that's why the song, *"Rest in Peace"* is included.

Edward Milano

Live Album Review

DELIVERIN'

BY: POCO

I listened to this on vinyl and it still delivers, despite the fact it was released in 1971. I won't go into a long history lesson about the historical relationship of Buffalo Springfield, CSNY, The Eagles, and Poco. It's an interesting story and in the end it seems Poco got the short end of the stick in the annals of country rock.

I think Poco was the anti-CSNY. Where CSNY came off as political and serious, Poco was optimistic and fun.

This set, recorded in Boston, featured Jim Messina, Richard Furay, Timothy Schmitt, James Grantham and Rusty Young. They were young and hungry.

The band is tight, the harmony's blend, and it sounds as if the band is having as much fun on stage as the audience is participating in this event. I'm sure battle lines were being drawn by the fans as to who was the best country rock band, and judging from the response, Poco was clearly on their way up. Too bad, in-fighting, control issues and musical direction would doom this assembly of musicians. The Eagles' need for bass players that can sing, of course, didn't help matters. This album today is the ghost of what might have been.

Live Album Review

JOURNEY TO THE CENTER OF THE EARTH

BY: RICK WAKEMAN

The original plan was to turn this live performance into a studio album, but the high costs made them choose a live performance instead. It played out to be a good move. Rick Wakeman was a rock star. In 1974, the band he played keyboards for was a supergroup of the progressive world. YES was at the top of their game, and climbing higher. Rick Wakeman was prolific enough by himself, and was limited playing in an ensemble. *JOURNEY TO THE CENTER OF THE EARTH* is a musical he wrote based on the Jules Verne classic book. Up till then, joining an orchestra and a rock band didn't have a very good track record. Jon Lord and Deep Purple tried it with Malcolm Arnold and Frank Zappa with Zubin Mehta. The results were less than stellar.

This record was a gamble, and it paid off. Rick Wakeman became more than a rock star. It has sold over 14 million units to date. Not bad for a 'crummy' keyboard player

Edward Milano

in a rock band. The music here is nothing like YES. I like the fact that Wakeman doesn't overdo his keyboard flourishes. He adds color when needed. This was a legitimate score and with an orchestra, vocalists, narration and rock band... it worked. I still enjoy listening to this even decades later. It's timeless, I feel as though I should dress in formal attire when I listen to it. Too bad Wakeman wore his lame silver cape during this performance. It must be a keyboardist thing, that and his reputation for eating onstage.

Live Album Review

EXIT STAGE LEFT

BY: RUSH

The band RUSH is a matter of individual taste. If you like them, it doesn't mean you have bad taste. If you dislike them, it doesn't mean you have good taste. That being said, this album is for people that like RUSH. 1981 is a long time ago, and they were veterans then. What does that make them today? I happen to like RUSH. Are they my favorite band of all time? No, not even in the top 50, but I like them anyway.

This live album is more of a showcase for the people on the fence that RUSH were every bit as good as the popular mega groups with half the talent. Nevermind the seriousness of their approach and the Sci-Fi/Ayn Rand lyrics, Geddy Lee's bass playing mingled in with synth, Alex Lifeson's guitar virtuoso, and Neil Peart's incredible drumming show that yes, they could actually play in concert what was on the studio records.

Geddy Lee's voice takes some getting used to (Maybe

that's why they never were considered cool, Geddy Lee just didn't sing or look like a rock star). They cover their history up to this point in their career. They deliver the songs with exact precision. Some are complicated, some are just good, radio friendly hits. "*The Spirit Of Radio*" and "*Tom Sawyer*" are expected fan favorites. The crowd singing along with "*Closer To The Heart*" shows that RUSH had a loyal following, despite critical disdain. "*Trees*", "*Xanadu*", and "*Jacobs Ladder*" are early prog rock which shows just how influential they were. Proggers today cite RUSH as a major influence."*La Villa Strangiato*" is the tune almost all aspiring guitarists learn. If you can learn to play that, you can play anything.

To me, "*Red Barchetta*" is the song that captivated me. I actually researched 'before the internet' what a Barchetta (Italian word for little boat) was. I bet their "*Red Barchetta*" could beat Prince's "*Little Red Corvette*" in a drag race. The song is still my favorite RUSH song, what's yours?

Live Album Review

THE GOLDEN AGE OF ROCK AND ROLL

BY: SHA NA NA

Now we're talking about some serious music here. Bill Graham introduces them to the crowd at The Winterland as, "The heavies from The Big Apple in the East." Heavy they are.. This is when Sha Na Na were badass. This album, *THE GOLDEN AGE OF ROCK AND ROLL* released in 1973. I still have the original vinyl on the Karma Sutra label with the great black and white poster that I have never tacked up. That and the gatefold photo show a bunch of ugly dudes that a nice girl wouldn't take home to meet her parents.

These boys played it to the hilt. Was it an act? Sure it was, considering some were college graduates, and some went on to have careers as doctors, lawyers and CEO's. These guys were no dummies but if they were acting, they should all get awards. Forget the homogenized version you saw on television. This is the original version, and they play and sing with the passion and energy of punk rockers. Face it, they were greasers, and that translates to punks with attitude.

Their song selection isn't teddy bears crying in the chapel, it's the nasty stuff. Songs with the double meanings: *"Hound Dog"*, *"Rock Around The Clock"*, *"Sea Cruise"*, *"Great Balls Of Fire"*, *"Shake, Rattle And Roll"*, *"Runaround Sue"*, *"Whole Lotta Shakin' Goin' On"* It's greasy, sweaty, sloppy, and I like it.

Three sides of this double album is live music, for they include a section of studio stuff that is good, but doesn't have the fire of a concert performance. I would have loved to see them at this early time in their career when they were young and put on such a great stage show. They were at Woodstock, believe it or not. I did see them at a state fair once, around the time of their television show, and I was disappointed. The only great memory I can take from it was Bowser saying to someone in the crowd, "What? What did you say? How would youse like a knuckle sandwich?" If that's the best memory from that show, then I'll stick to listening to this album. I recommend you do too if you want to hear Sha Na Na when they really deliver knuckle sandwiches.

LIVE!

BY: STATUS QUO

A rock band that sells 120 million records has to be one of the biggest and most popular bands in history. The Beatles? No. The Rolling Stones? No, again. Well then, Led Zeppelin or The Who? No! Pink Floyd? Stop guessing, you're not even warm.

Status Quo. I repeat, Status Quo, to allow it to sink in. Big in England, where they have become an institution. It's a good thing people there buy records and go to shows, because these guys couldn't get arrested in The United States.

STATUS QUO LIVE! is a double album, released in 1977. Recorded, from a gig in Glasgow, Scotland. The 'Frantic Four' of Francis Rossi on guitar and vocals, Rick Parfitt on guitar and vocals, Alan Lancaster on bass and vocals and John Coghlan on drums are present and accounted for. They have two auxiliary members; Andy Brown on keyboards, and Bob Young on harmonica to help fatten the sound. They must be what Ian Stewart was to The Stones: too ugly to be a shareholder.

I jest and it doesn't make a bit of difference because the four principal members play as if they are the middle child in the rock and roll boogie family. Slade would be the filthy youngest, who dipped themselves in glitter to make it in the business. Fogat would have to be the entitled eldest, for they had Rod Price and they played it louder and included blues in their repertoire.

Status Quo is the middle child. I doubt they said, "Foghat, Foghat, Foghat," to protest the success and attention the older child was getting. They didn't need to. They had a gang of friends, all their own, who, by golly, liked them. So, why sweat about the ugly Americans? Status Quo has 120 million reasons to let it roll off their back and into their bank. Let's go to The Apollo in Glasgow and check them out.

Before Status Quo pile drives them into boogie submission, a warm announcement is made to the Glasgow crowd. "*Junior's Waiting*" is fast, hard, and a great opener. The crowd is present and just as loud as the band. "*Backwater/Just Take Me*" are two interlocked songs, which seem to be what Status Quo likes to do in concert.

"*Backwater*" starts out as Southern Rock before the boogie takes over. Without a pause they roll into, "*Just Take Me*". Both songs are obvious fan favorites, from the response

Live Album Review

the band is getting, which is thunderous appreciation. This combination of songs works well for Status Quo so they do it throughout their show and that's what this album is all about: Status Quo in concert, where the audience is expected to participate.

I like this stuff. It's not the familiar stuff Yanks in the 70s pounded their heads to, but it's solid, well played Chuck Berry on steroids, rock and roll. If Chuck's songs seemed to be recycled 'Johnny B. Goode' then Status Quo has created their special noise by studying from the master. It is three chords and a cloud of dust. Does it matter if they're the same three chords? Ask Angus and Malcom Young.

Status Quo likes to let everybody in on a little secret that there's more to them than meets the ears. Many songs will begin with a tasty, dual guitar melody from Rossi and Parfitt, that reminds one of Wishbone Ash. Just when they suck you in, they body slam you with the boogie and they are masters of it. They can stretch a song with the best of them. *"Forty-Five Hundred Times"* is close to seventeen minutes of a band doing what they want, till they don't want to do it anymore. That's the best I can do to describe it. It takes some skill to change tempos and lower the volume without missing a beat, only to bring everything back to a furious gallop. The rhythm section stays steady as Rossi and Parfitt play guitar solos, power chords or just verbally interact with the audience, who are just as much part of the show as the band. I see why Status Quo planted their flag and staked their claim on British soil: the people. The band members were jean clad, long-haired and hardworking. You could tell from the photos, they had the rock star poses down to a science, which only made them cooler. When they play songs like, *"Don't Waste My Time"*, and *"Is There A Better Way?"* they are playing anthems. The audience sings right along or gang chants, in soccer, hooliganism fashion. This band knows their people and is more than happy to give them what they want.

I want to listen to this album, loud in my car. I'm not sure how I would have felt at an actual show in the 1970s. Status Quo is good, but so were many, many bands that opened for the 'Big Names'. I guess it's because I was born in the U.S.A. and liked Foghat. Chances are I would have loved it. Why play short sets for short money in the states? I don't blame them one bit and applaud their longevity.

People say that the creators of Spinal Tap took a lot of inspiration from Status Quo. There are some similarities, like the early psychedelia of *"Pictures of Matchstick Men"*, and a song found here, *"Big Fat Mama"*. In all fairness to Status Quo, there's no joke about their fourteen minute take on *"Roadhouse Blues"*. Including this may have been an effort to enlighten Americans, but alas, the over-the-top blues harmonica, as the band tear through this version that slams the

Live Album Review

door on Jim Morrison and company. Next to Frank Marino, I haven't heard a better live performance of this song from a classic rock concert that's as real as real can get. That ain't bad....that's good. You get limitless energy, singing and yelling, hand clapping, guitar solos, drum solos and pounding, boogie riffs that make you want to play some air guitar.

The band put this album out, warts and all. I don't feel any warts, just goosebumps from time-to-time. It was non-stop rock for over 90 minutes before boogie got hijacked by disco.

Edward Milano

Live Album Review

ALIVE IN AMERICA

BY: STEELY DAN

What a great album cover. The music isn't bad either.

In 1993-94 Donald Fagen and Walter Becker graced us with their presence on stage. They hadn't toured as Steely Dan since 1974, when 'The Dan' was an actual band. Here, studio pros surround them, bringing the cerebral cynicism in polished, jazz-infused perfection. It doesn't matter who they are, only that they are brilliant. Well, I guess it does matter to them,they are the ones playing the music and they do it in Steely Dan style.

This set was released in 1995, and people were hungry for it. Always the anti-heros of the pop industry, Walter and Donald didn't disappoint. Even if the song selection left much to be desired. In fairness, there isn't a bad Steely Dan song, so they could have picked anything from their history and it would have worked.

The opener of *"Babylon Sisters"* has that familiar cool vibe with space to let the soloists breathe. *"Green Earrings"* rolls directly into *"Bodhisattva'"* and the band is cooking. The guys have enough ammunition in their backing band to showcase themselves on their individual instruments.

Fagen has a great expressive feel on his keys and Becker plays a decent lead guitar. He's no Larry Carlton but who's listening that close?. In the past, he always seemed to be in the background, and in the early days let Skunk Baxter and Denny Dias handle the leads while he played bass. Here, it's evident he was more of a contributor than people may have given him credit for. While on the subject of lead guitar, *"REELIN' IN THE YEARS"* is a different animal from the classic studio version. The guys elect to feature horns running the classic lead patterns instead of the guitar. If it was anyone else, they wouldn't have gotten away with it, but this is Steely Dan. Their established reputation and hipster arrangements send them past 'Go, and collect $200.00'.

This is great stuff, and it's just getting started. *"Josie"*, *"Peg"*, *"Third World Man"*, *"Kid Charlemagne"*, and *"Sign In Stranger"* are all excellent readings, even if some would be considered 'deep tracks'.

"Book of Liars" is a Walter Becker tune from his solo album, *11 TRACKS OF WHACK*. His singing voice is reasonable, and it's curious to why he didn't sing more for Steely Dan. It may be because of the subject matter. Fagen's creepy uncle singing voice is perfect for the typical Steely Dan song,

Live Album Review

which is usually shrouded in mystery with some mild, sarcastic humor. This one is acerbic and directed at somebody Walter isn't fond of. Here's hoping he never gets mad at me.

The album closes with "*Aja*" that is beatnik cool. Listening to it makes me want to leave my socks at home, wear a scarf and sip some wine. It's the longest song on this set, as it should be for maximum effect. If not for the crowd noises and the title of the album, you might think this was a studio production. The sound is perfect (it's Steely Dan, why would I think otherwise?).When it all winds down, you want to hear more Steely Dan songs in this live format. I can think of eleven songs off the top of my head, other than the eleven songs they have on this. I can think of eleven more after that and after that.

Edward Milano

BRING ON THE NIGHT

BY: STING

You can say many things about Sting, but you can't say he's a dummy. This live set is from 1986 and it's representative of the space he was occupying at the time- Jazz. Was it crazy to leave the Police when they were at the apex? 20/20 Hindsight says "No", but at the time, it was open to debate. When I first heard this album, when it released, I fell in love with it. I'm still in love with it. At first, I was skeptical because his first couple of solo albums didn't impress me, but this live set grabbed me from the opening track *"Bring On The Night/When The World Is Running Down"*. He starts with a couple of Police tunes (he's no dummy), but this doesn't sound anything like The Police: it's eleven minutes of kick-ass jazz. And it would be considering who his backing band is Brandford Marsalis, Darryl Jones, Omar Hakim and Kenny Kirkland as well as incredible background singers. Here's some of the artists the band members have played with: Miles Davis, Wynton Marsalis, Weather Report, and Dizzy Gillespie. This band was the real-deal (I told you Sting is no

Live Album Review

dummy). They fill in the gaps of the music with so much color, it jumps at you. You can't sit down and listen to this and if you're up and moving, you have to dance to it. You can't help it, it's that effective. There's plenty of his solo stuff on this as well as other Police tunes. I appreciate the fact that they didn't include "*Roxanne*" and "*Every Step You Take*". We can hear those in every terrible nineties 'rom-com'.

Like I said before, you can't sit down and listen to this. It makes you wanna dance. I'm sure Sting didn't make any money on this tour for the wages he had to pay, but it was a smart career move. Let the band interpret the songs and let's have a party. Sting obviously is no slouch either, just to be able to share the stage with these musicians, but he shows he's more than capable of the challenge and I think that's what he needed -to be challenged again. The only small criticism I have is the rap that's included on the song "*When the World Is Running Down*". It's not necessary, and almost ruins the vibe by taking it to a level of commercial gratuity. It doesn't last long, and the groove makes it more like bird crap on the windshield that's quickly washed off. *BRING ON THE NIGHT* is the title, and in my opinion, it's still the best of Sting's solo work to date.

BROTHER BAND AT FILMORE EAST

BY: THE ALLMAN BROTHERS

The title says it all. No nonsense, to the point and on the money.

This would be the band's third album and would break them into the 'big time.' The original l.p. dropped in 1971, as a double album with only seven songs. Only seven? As if the customer would feel they were ripped off. There have been reissues and some of the material from the same series of Fillmore concerts ended up on the next album, *EAT A PEACH.*

So why did this one take off? Because it's great!

"Statesboro Blues", with Duane Allman's wicked slide work, starts it, and there's no let-up. *"Done Somebody Wrong"*, *"Stormy Monday"* and *"You Don't Love Me"* make up the first album. Duane Allman already had a great reputation at the time and had to pay the bills by doing session work. He would even play with Eric Clapton in Derek and Domi-

Live Album Review

noes. Little brother Greg sang with a voice decades beyond his age and played and coaxed the soul out of his organ.

It's this album that allowed Richard Betts to become a household name. He mixes it up with Duane and holds his own as a guitar player's guitar player. From a musician's perspective, there are albums you just listen to and albums you study and learn and/or steal from. This one is most certainly the latter. The two drummers play like they are 4 arms on the same body and Berry Oakley on bass, who, along with Duane, would soon be gone. Together they all were beyond everything else. They weren't hippies, but got played on the hippie FM stations. The second album from this set got worn out.

Honestly, the second album is what seals the deal. "Hot Lanta" followed by the now legendary, "In Memory Of Elizabeth Reed". It's that song alone that separated them from the pack of guitar based, blues bands. Rock, jazz fusion, and blues with a southern accent. Forget the rambling of the Grateful Dead; these guys owned their instruments and didn't allow drugs to open doors to places where the music would roam. No way, The Allman brothers were disciplined. Instead of acid, they let Anheuser Busch take the edge off. If you didn't have this, a friend did. If you didn't borrow it, somebody borrowed yours. If you didn't listen to it on 8-track, in the car, while passing a joint, you missed out.

As mentioned earlier, there have been reissues containing more songs, more information, and it's all well and good. For me, the original, on vinyl, is all you need. 8 Track, reel to reel, cassette or even CD would suffice but regardless, the format, the seven songs here is all you need. Anything else would ruin the perfect vibe. In fact, this album is considered culturally important enough to be in the Library Of Congress.

It's comforting to know that after The Zombie Apocalypse, The Allman Brothers will survive for the reconstruction. Maybe that's why a twenty-three minute version of "*Whipping Post*" ends this set.

Live Album Review

LIVE! AT THE BBC

BY: THE BEATLES

LIVE! AT THE BBC released in 1994, some 30 years after these recordings (1963-65) broadcast on various music, and variety shows from the BBC. This was in the old days, so artists were at the mercy of the monolith. Over 56 songs are on this and Beatle fans, no doubt, had no problem letting the APPLE machine print more money. Hearing this, you can tell The Beatles were a great bar band.

The Beatles covered Motown, Rockabilly, Blues, Rock and Roll, Show tunes and Country and Western. The resemblance to The Nashville Cats is actually quite striking. George certainly studied from the book of Scotty Moore and Carl Perkins. Chuck Berry stuff they do okay, but The Stones obviously did it better. What's missing is a piano. Why they didn't add one to the band when they were developing their sound, I don't know. The Stones had Ian Stewart on the side, banging the keys. Paul sings Little Richard and Elvis Presley like a true protégé, but then can sing a slower number ever so sweetly. They do the song *"Clarabella"* that Paul sings great. It's blues and they are walking in territory most British bands were exploring. They obviously are adept and pull it off, but it's clear it's not what they want to do full time.

The Beatles were a jukebox. What's interesting is listening to their originals on this set. They mesh so perfectly because you can tell all the influences from their covers carried over into the songs they wrote, arranged, performed, and sang. Before the broadcast, they pre-recorded this music but performed it live. This music would work well in a small setting. I guess it didn't matter because when they played arenas and stadiums, you couldn't hear over the screaming anyway. The Beatles were learning and were just students when they recorded this album stuff. When they graduated later, they became teachers, and others would learn from them. When they became masters, they burned out, but what a career!

Live Album Review

CONCERT FOR BANGLADESH

BY: GEORGE HARRISON

THE CONCERT FOR BANGLADESH, Come on George. You released a triple album in 1970 and now you're dropping another one on us in 1971. Nevermind, it's for charity and it won a Grammy. A Madison Square Garden, star-studded event that paved the way for more benefits of this nature. Thanks George. You're not the Quiet Beatle anymore.

The history is in the archives, so Phil Spector's Wall of Sound, ABKCO piracy and critical lashing can be researched on your own because the real question remains to who has listened to the album in its entirety? I saw the movie at least three times, if my memory is intact. I even have it stashed away somewhere in my things but honestly, I never listened to the actual three record album (that I have stashed away) from start to finish. I would rather watch paint dry than listen to Ravi and his sitar that requires, "Concentrated Listening" and "No Smoking.." If I get through that, then I can enjoy an almost Beatle reunion.

Ringo is here, so that's two Beatles. Paul was invited but wasn't feeling the love. John boycotted because Yoko wasn't invited. Good... Not good because John didn't lend his talents, but good because Yoko didn't lend hers. Billy Preston is here, and he played on some Beatle tracks from *LET IT BE*. Eric Clapton's body is here and he also played with the band on *THE WHITE ALBUM*. Klaus Voorman is here, and he's part of The Beatles Hamburg legend. He designed the *REVOLVER* album cover and knows Astrid personally. I guess that qualifies him to play bass. Why? is anyone's guess. You tell me nobody else was available? Keef would have done it. He played with The Dirty Mac, didn't he?

My decision to listen to the whole six sides was not without fear. Could I do it? If I couldn't, then would I not be cool, like the kids on that National Lampoon album, *RADIO DINNER*, that loved George because he spreads himself so thickly over the earth. Under this pressure, I had to give it a go.

It starts with applause as George Harrison welcomes the crowd. Ravi Shankar sounds like he's having a bad day when he talks to the audience while tuning up. He and his band go on to play "*Bangla Dhun*". Ravi is one of the greats on sitar. My Western ears still can't tell if he made any mistakes. I admit to zoning out during the course of his musi-

Live Album Review

cal journey. It sure didn't sound much different then what George did on "Within You, Without You". I caught myself singing the lyrics while listening to some of the 17 minute examples of "real," Indian Music. And someone said rock and roll all sounded the same. If there's a top ten list of the greatest sitar players, I reckon Ravi Shankar is there, somewhere.

"Wah Wah" gets the crowd up and cheering. George Harrison and Friends have hit the stage. His singing voice is weak and the band sounds big. Two drummers, Ringo and Jim Keltner, and George, Eric and Jesse Ed Davis handle the electric guitars. Pete Ham, Tom Evans and Joey Molland of Badfinger play acoustic guitars. Billy Preston and Leon Russell play keyboards. The Hollywood Horns are in the house, as well as The Soul Choir. Much of this is Leon Russell's doing, so let's say he had a hand in making the music what it was.

"My Sweet Lord" is played fast, George has a real case of the nerves as he sings it with little passion. Eric, well, I don't hear him doing much.

"Awaiting On You All" is not the best George Harrison song, but it's his show. Again, where's Eric? If you didn't know he was there, you wouldn't know he was there. Heroin and "I'm in love with your wife, George" don't seem to be helping.

Billy Preston brings some life into the proceedings

with "*That's the Way God Planned It*". I remember his performance in the movie, so that picture helps with what I'm hearing.

Ringo shouts his solo hit of "*It Don't Come Easy*" and the audience loves it. I can't say it was great, but it's passable. No wonder The Beatles didn't want to play live besides Paul.

"*Beware of Darkness*" kind of puts a damper on the energy. Leon contributes to the singing of this and after the whole song is performed, it turns out to be one of the better tunes from this show.

"*While My Guitar Gently Weeps*" should have featured some stellar guitar work by Eric Clapton, but it doesn't. There's no fire in his solo or any additional licks he throws in. What does it matter? This is for charity. The rest of the people on stage bring the noise to make it work.

Leon Russell, with some additional players, bangs out the medley of "*Jumpin' Jack Flash/Youngblood*". Now this is a spark that's been missing. Leon knows what he's doing, and this is no different from his traveling circus. I would say he's stealing the show, but there's not much, so far, to steal.

George returns with his acoustic guitar to play and sing, "*Here Comes the Sun*". Good stuff, and it's a primer for what's next, which would be the killer of the whole set, in the person of Bob Dylan. George assists on electric guitar and Leon plays bass. You didn't think Klaus was going to be given that task?

Live Album Review

"A Hard Rain's Gonna Fall", *"It Takes A Lot to Laugh"*, *"It Takes a Train to Cry"*, *"Blowin' In the Wind"*, *"Mr. Tambourine Man"* and *"Just Like a Woman"*. Bob is singing nasally, clear, and blows his harmonica like he always did. Not bad for a guy who hasn't been onstage for two years. I read somewhere that he had cold feet until the 11th hour. I wonder what was Plan B? Eric didn't do any songs. Badfinger didn't do any. Bob showed up, and for me, is the highlight of the whole album.

George Harrison ends the show with *"Something"* and the song he wrote for this event, *"Bangladesh"*. It's all over now, baby blue. Bob didn't sing that one, but could have ended the concert with it. The song *"Bangladesh"* is a call for action. *"Give some bread"* isn't the kind you eat. It's cash. It was an expensive gesture to put this show together and Allen Klein didn't help matters any. By the time they sorted it all out, they sent little money to the people it was intended for. It sounded like a good idea. I do know that continued sales of this album and concert movie have generated a few million for the cause. I don't know if the cause is still the same, but it's still for charity, not ABKCO.

That being said, I listened to the whole album in one sitting. I wasn't in a lotus position, but was reclined. It's not the best live album I've ever heard, but it's not the worst. The assembly of talent creates an illusion that the music would be spectacular. It's just average. Watching the movie helps a great deal.

Edward Milano

Live Album Review

IT'S ALIVE

BY: THE RAMONES

It's New Year's Eve in London in 1977 and the Ramones are playing at The Rainbow Theatre. This particular show was considered the best of the tour and at its conclusion, some of the crowd thought it proper to pull up the seats in the venue and throw them on the stage. I don't know the actual story and if this occurred at all. Hype and over-exaggeration goes a long way for promotional purposes. The live album pulled from this show, *IT'S ALIVE* was released in 1979. By then the group had established themselves and Punk Rock was weeding out the fakers.

Next to The Beatles, I can't think of any group that was more influential. Today, Punk Rock is an accepted musical genre but in 1977 it sounded ugly, played by people that were ugly in dress, manners and talent. I think the Ramones were as surprised at their success as anyone, for what started out as a joke turned into a movement.

IT'S ALIVE is twenty-eight songs of rude energy. The

set is fast and there is little space between the songs, other than, "one, two, three, four." It's amazing anyone in the band could count that high, considering the stories, but the "*Cretin Hop*" is just part of the act.

I admit to being fascinated by them when they first broke and preferred them to anything Disco. I sure didn't stake my reputation on their abilities or argue they were better than anyone else. Who did this stuff anyway? I was wrong and sure Jimmy Page could play guitar better than Johnny Ramone but so can I. That means nothing to the crowd at The Rainbow and Jimmy Page was a dinosaur that can stick his Les Paul up his bum. The Ramones are what it's about now and they are leading the blitzkrieg of anarchy.

The original gang is here: Joey Ramone on vocals, Johnny Ramone on guitar, Dee Dee Ramone on bass and Tommy Ramone on drums. They begin with "*Rockaway Beach*" and end with "*We're A Happy Family*". In between they are glue sniffing commandos that need shock treatment. Judy, Suzy and Sheena are here and they can make one well with a lobotomy.

This album has been declared one of the best live albums ever. When it comes to declarations of greatness, I always wonder who's passing out these awards and what makes them so smart? I don't care because the Ramones never claimed to be smart, cool, or good. They just couldn't

Live Album Review

do anything else and sure weren't going to work a day job. I think they had more going on than people gave them credit for and "*Here Today, Gone Tomorrow*" didn't come true, now did it?

If you haven't heard this, then what are you waiting for? It's raw, unfiltered and ugly. I love it. I knew a dude at the time, who wasn't ready for it, described The Ramones as, " the worst S#$@ I ever heard in my life." This guy liked the band America, and if he hated the Ramones, then that gave me more reason to like them. If it ticked him off when I played it, then the Ramones did their job.

LIVE AT LEEDS

BY: THE WHO

This is the best live album ever. There are many that can sit at second place on the list but this one stands alone at the top of the heap. A desert island disc of four trains converging in the same place at the same time and they still managed to make it work. How? Nobody knows and that's what made the Who special. No detailed review is needed. If you don't have it, then get it and play it loud.

Live Album Review

AROUND THE WORLD WITH THREE DOG NIGHT

BY: THREE DOG NIGHT

What would you say about a band that had multiple, number-one hit singles, sold out every stop on their tours, had multiple number one albums and sold a bazillion records? You would say that the band would rank up there with The Beatles, unless you say the name Three Dog Night, then the knives come out. I never understood this. Sure, they didn't write their own material, but neither did Elvis. They weren't The Monkees either, but somehow The Monkees got more love than 3DN and The Dawgs could sing and play their instruments.

This double live album from 1973 is when the band was peaking. I could list all the songs, but it would just sound like a greatest hits package. What's nice about this set is that it's a band, not some hired hands. They arranged their songs and vocals and put much work into their act. They were tight, with an edge of sloppiness. The performances are live without a net. Goofing around sometimes and interacting with the audience, the three vocalists are great showmen. I guarantee if you listen to the song *"Midnight Runaway"* without knowing who it was, you would say the band and singer are great... because they were. Many budding songwriters at the time can thank 3DN for covering their songs and getting their name out there: Elton John, Paul Williams, John Hiatt, Hoytt Axton, Laura Nyro, Harry Nilsson, Russ Ballard. They even did an obscure Lennon/McCartney tune that certainly made people go back and check out the original.

BUT, getting back to the album, it rocks, jams, and it's sweet in places. It certainly brings back memories. Vinyl albums were always fun because of the art work, the pictures and the liner notes. This album is full of them and you can listen while reading and perusing the gatefold and the record sleeves. The music is fun. *"Old Fashioned Love Song"* is a classic. *"Joy to the World"* is imprinted on the world. Just those two songs alone would make a band's career and these were just two of many and there are many to be heard here.

The Rock and Roll Hall Of Fame has purposely snubbed 3DN. They should get in just for being The Rat Pack of their generation. These were no choir boys, and like the pack, they partied. The only difference is the drugs, and they did eventually take their toll on the band. Jimmy Green-

Live Album Review

spoon and Chuck Negron both have books detailing the rise and fall. Believe me... they outgunned Guns and Roses. It's great they were able to document their live show before the decline. In retrospect,they should have named this album, BEFORE THE FALL.

WINGS OVER AMERICA

BY: WINGS

(Not yet, Sir) Paul McCartney has arrived. Forget The Beatles This is Macca and Wings (Laine, McCulloch, English, Linda, and a horn section). They played a world tour, filling stadiums and arenas on the strength of hit albums, hit singles, and plenty of press. This set, released in 1976, was pulled from selected shows in the U.S.A. McCartney's sound engineer reportedly listened to every concert and picked the best performances to hand off to Paul, who then went and did some studio tweaking. Always an opportunist, the "America" idea was more than coincidental in 1976.

I appreciate the fact that the album's title doesn't lead with Paul McCartney's name. His confidence was high, and he wanted to make the point that Wings were a band that he was a member of. I'm not buying it but still appreciate that his band had reached a point that it was popular and recognizable enough to sell products without his name. He was still competing, and this drove him to reach higher, if for any-

Live Album Review

thing to prove to the ex-Beatles, the music critics and John Lennon fans that he really was good.

Who cares? At this point in his career, Paul McCartney was an established superstar who used to play in that other band. He demonstrates this by opening with *"Venus and Mars/Rock Show/Jet"*. This ain't the mop tops. This is all Paul, and the song is a concert in itself. *"Let Me Roll It"* is next, and it sounds like Paul McCartney and The Plastic Ono Band. *"Spirits of Ancient Egypt"* could have been left off, but Denny Laine gets a lead vocal here. Paul also gives Jimmy McCulloch an early spotlight on *"Medicine Jar"*, an anti-drug song, sadly ironic in retrospect, given McCulloch's later death from overdose. It rocks and Jimmy shows off his talents as a lead guitarist.

With side one down, Paul elects to play some piano on side two. *"Maybe I'm Amazed"*, *"Call Me Back Again"*, *"Lady Madonna"*, (Huh? a Beatles song?) *"The Long and Winding Road"* (another Beatle song), and the big production number of *"Live and Let Die"*. Whew, this already is enough to send everyone home happy, and it's just getting started!

An acoustic set starts side three and Paul, on acoustic guitar, does *"Picasso's Last Words"*, *"Bluebird"*, *"I've Just Seen a Face"*, *"Blackbird"* and *"Yesterday"* (more Beatles songs, come on Paul). So far, Paul has played bass, piano, acoustic guitar, and sang most of the songs. He's a pretty talented guy and there's still half a concert to go.

"*You Gave Me The Answer*", "*Magneto*" and "*Titanium Man*", "*Go Now*" (Denny singing his big hit with The Moody Blues in the sixties). The great ones of "*My Love*" and "*Listen To What the Man Said*". The horn section is out now and it works. It's clear that Paul knows how to pace a concert set list. He plays his "fantastic songs" after a couple of marginal ones. I would have preferred more of his earlier solo work, but I wasn't asked. On with the show....

"*Let 'em In*" is intended as a bicentennial salute. "*Silly Love Songs*" knocks the crowd off their feet. For such a simple tune, McCartney overcomes the critics by making it a showcase. This would be a perfect closer, but Paul wants to rock. So much for him being a lightweight. He and Wings are out to prove they can be as aggressive as the other arena gods of the day. I may have included songs such as "*Junior's Farm*" and "*Helen Wheels*", but sadly again, I wasn't asked. They do play "*Beware My Love*", "*Letting Go*", "*Band on The Run*", "*Hi, Hi, Hi*" and the unreleased "*Soily*" which is a great rocker. I never understood why Paul would leave great material on the shelf instead of using them to make his studio albums better.

Wow! Like him or hate him, this live album is impressive. Some have said this is the best Wings line-up, and listening to how tight and professional they sound, I would

Live Album Review

agree. Paul put much thought into this record, from the Hipnosis cover to the inside sleeve info and photos, to the poster, not to mention the abundance of music. Just think of the songs he didn't play. One interesting note is that all Beatle songs here are listed as McCartney/Lennon compositions. I guess releasing a triple album from a successful tour wasn't enough for Paul. One would think having the record chart and selling millions would be vindication. I guess a subtle twist of the knife to John, who was in the midst of his "lost weekend."

YESSONGS

BY: YES

Due to the recent snub of the band YES by The Rock and Roll Hall of 'Shame', I felt it necessary to review one of their live albums. *YESSONGS* was released in 1973; a triple album, which in those days was pricey. Roger Dean's artwork is all over it, with the continuing theme of the exploding planet fragments drifting through space to find a home on some water world. The actual story is told on Jon Anderson's excellent solo album, *OLIAS OF SUNHILLOW*.

Anyway, this live set was recorded before technology caught up to the band. To recreate their studio work on stage, in large arenas was not easy in the early seventies. Their later live albums would offer a more pristine sound but it's not important here. *YESSONGS* features the band everyone knows and loves: Anderson, Wakeman, Howe, Squire and White. The original drummer, Bill Bruford is represented on a few tracks, which is a good thing. Sound wise, it's not perfect and does have an echo at times, but it feels like

Live Album Review

you are really listening to the band in a hockey rink with bad acoustics. Every instrument is isolated and you can clearly hear what each member is playing to create the unique sound of Yes. Forget the studio embellishments and overdubs this is four musicians and a vocalist performing the songs and they do it well.

The opening *"Firebird Suite"* sounds like canned music. The band launches into *"Siberian Khatru"* and they play it note perfect. Perfect as a live performance can be. Sure, there's some missed notes and off key singing, but it harms nothing. This isn't easy music to play and sing. I like the fact that the band released this stuff, warts and all. It's real and you appreciate just how good they are because of it.

"Heart of the Sunrise" is next, and it's amazing how clear Chris Squire's bass work cuts through the musical arrangement. Jon Anderson's voice is clear, strong and is fun to listen to because, as mentioned earlier, every instrument is isolated and you can focus on each player. Those who studied the big three: *THE YES ALBUM, FRAGILE* and *CLOSE TO THE EDGE* will know what I mean. Those are, in many opinions, their finest period, and songs from those three albums are what are played on *YESSONGS*.

"Perpetual Change" is one of the performances that featured Bill Bruford's drums. On this he solos, but not after the band performs the song. The vocal harmonies resolve

well, despite the fact that Squire and Howe don't really have good voices, but they do have good pitch control and they certainly mesh well with Jon Anderson's choirboy vocals.

"YOU AND I" is the only song on this whole album that the band has trouble pulling off. I'm surprised they even attempted it, but regardless, it's still pretty credible. Steve Howe performs a classical guitar feature "Mood for a Day", which sounds excellent of course, his playing is stellar. Rick Wakeman gets a solo spot with excerpts from "THE SIX WIVES OF HENRY VIII". Personally, I could have done without this. I'm not sure why his solo album needed plugging here since this is a Yes show. I would have preferred another Yes song, but maybe the others needed to rest their fingers and voices. Nonetheless, it's amazing what he can achieve because the instruments he used and the sounds he produced were revolutionary, not to mention costly. I'm sure his keyboard setup took up half the stage. Today, it would fit on a laptop computer.

The band returns to perform "Roundabout". It's lively and rocks, for YES anyway. You have to put up with Howe playing electric guitar on the whole song, even the technical harmonics, but he pulls it off. It's really fun to hear Squire's weaving bass lines and Wakeman's synth flourishes. Each person had a specific pattern to follow to make it work. It's incredible that they could do it. The duo of "Your Move" and

Live Album Review

"All Good People" are probably the best representation of the band. They nail the vocal arrangements and when the band takes off, it's a perfect performance of one of the perfect songs ever written. Listening to it makes me mad at The Beatles. They were reluctant to play live after 1966 because, other than the crowd noise, they said they couldn't reproduce their studio work on stage. YES, in this song, prove that you can. Rehearsal, caring about your fans and hard work are the key ingredients.

"Long Distance Runaround" is another song featuring Bill Bruford and you can clearly distinguish his style from Alan Whites. The band, with Bruford, goes directly into *"The Fish"*. It's a different animal from the Squire instrumental on *FRAGILE*. There is some playful interplay between Squire, and Bruford. Howe adds some color, and Wakeman keeps it together with his background keys. Nice work. Bruford wanted the band to play loser, which is probably why he left. The song "Close To the Edge" is performed in its entirety. It still amazes me. I can listen to it 100 times and still hear something new. The song, *"Yours Is No Disgrace"* starts out with some piano and steel guitar fun by Wakeman and Howe. It just sets up the grand intro to the song before the vocalists take it from there. You, as a listener, can just feel the intense emotion.

"Starship Trooper" ends this triple album, and it's the

closest the band gets to psychedelic music. The ending section is trippy, and it builds and carries on much longer than the studio version. I'm sure they could have played all night, but you already got three albums worth of music, so be content and go home happy.

This is well worth a listen, if anything, just to say they're better than Kiss.

Live Album Review

Edward Milano

Live Album Review

ZAPPA/MOTHERS ROXY AND ELSEWHERE

BY: ZAPPA

Today was a very difficult day and blasting this album aided greatly in bringing a smile to my face and a spring in my step.

ZAPPA/MOTHERS ROXY and ELSEWHERE is my favorite Zappa album but I'm biased because the band on this set is, in my opinion, the best band Frank Zappa ever had.

How's this for a backing band? Napoleon Murphy Brock, Chester Thompson, George Duke, Ruth Underwood, Jeff Simmons and brothers Tom and Bruce Fowler. Jean Luc Ponty was in this band but left prior to this recording. Every song is a classic and even if you're not a Zappa fan, you can't not like this (how can one dislike Cheepnis?). Jazz fusion was popular in 1974 and Frank jumped on the bandwagon in an attempt to get his "cruddy" music on the radio and increase sales.

Edward Milano

There's great singing, great ensemble playing, great soloing and loads and loads of Frank Zappa's guitar. Humor is everywhere and you can tell Zappa's having a blast interacting with the band and the crowd. The cover depicts an audience participation segment and the girl's hand is not in Frank's pants. He enjoyed controlling and conducting people to "Freak Out." He was fascinated with social engineering and the science of crowd manipulation. Some of this is shown in a movie called 'Dub Room Special' that's interspersed with claymation from Bruce Bickford. It's a trip.... and Frank didn't do drugs. Legend is Ruth Underwood stripped during her percussive solo from this album. I'm not buying that story and I'm sure it originated with Frank, who advised Alice Cooper, early in his career, to not tell anyone he didn't tear a chicken apart onstage because the people "love it."

False propaganda can make a legend, like Frank eating S&*% onstage. Suffice to say, there is not a speck of S%^# on this album. Opening with, *"Penguin in Bondage"*, Frank chats up the audience before he and the band take them on a fun-filled, jazz- fusion romp to the far reaches of interplanetary travel that doesn't end till the double album closes with, a hard one to play, *"Be-Bop Tango"* (Of The Old Jazzmen's Church). Zappa carefully doctored this set in the studio and the sound quality is pristine.

A later release of this band can be found on *YOU*

Live Album Review

CAN'T DO THAT ON STAGE ANYMORE THE HELSINKI CON-CERT. It was not doctored with, so you get a full show, warts and all, with the same cast of characters. For my money, this one stands as one of Frank Zappa's best, along with *HOT RATS* and *JOE'S GARAGE*.

After that, you're on your own.

YARDBIRDS FIVE LIVE!

BY: YARDBIRDS

In 1964, there was a British rock and roll boom happening. The Beatles breaking in America was a big reason. When that happened, record companies were scouting English bands, looking for their next big thing. The Yardbirds were one of those bands who already had a reputation and a devoted following, playing American rhythm and blues, with much the same repertoire as everyone else. There are many reasons for that but, in those days, watching the competition was the best way to get material. If the crowd responded favorably to a song, then by jove, we can do a rave-up of it. "Rave-Up" was just another way of saying "jamming" or "free-form improvisation."

The Yardbirds, who in 1964, were Keith Relf on lead vocals and harmonica, Paul Samwell-Smith on bass, Chris Dreja on rhythm guitar, Jim McCarthy on drums and Eric Clapton on lead guitar, were a band that popularized the Rave-Up. Instead of just playing a song for three minutes,

Live Album Review

they were prone to extend it for five or six minutes. Having the guitar skills of Eric Clapton and the harp talents of Keith Relf enabled them to do it. That, and the fact that they were louder than everybody else, got them noticed and signed to a recording contract. *FIVE LIVE YARDBIRDS* is their debut album that was dropped on time for Christmas of 1964. It was a gamble but on stage is where they were at their best. It didn't sell and because of that, it didn't get released in America. They were too good or just too pure in their covers.

Rave-Ups were great in a club, but on record, I don't think the record buying masses were ready. Today, it's a seminal album and one of the earliest recorded documents of Eric Clapton. This gig is stated as being at The Marquee Club in London. After an introduction that includes a shout out to each member of the band, *"Too Much Monkey Business"* is played. This is not any different from versions of other bands from this time period. Eric Clapton is there, but not in front. You can identify his style and his subtle additions in-between the music. No blazing solo or crying blue licks. *"I Got Love If You Want It"* is next and again, more of the same musical arrangement as you've heard others play. Keith Relf can blow that harmonica and it seems like he's the one the focus is on. The Rolling Stones have their Jagger and the Yardbirds have their Relf.

"Smokestack Lightin" is reported to be one of their

more popular and requested tunes from the stage and here it's documented as to why. The Yardbirds demonstrate a proper Rave-Up on this one. Dreja and Clapton are locked in together like The Stones' art of weaving with Richards and Jones. The Rhythm section is not just in the pocket, they are providing a noisy backdrop as Keith Relf is shouting and playing his harp. The band rock the blues on this one and that sinister Howlin' Wolf blues feel is recreated and stretched into a jam. That is more about the band playing the music as a unit than individuals playing solos. They feed off the crowd and get more powerful as they progress.

"Good Morning Little Schoolgirl" has Paul Samwell-Smith and Eric Clapton singing as a duo. This must also be one of the earliest recordings of Clapton singing. He's not very confident, which is probably why Samwell-Smith is singing as well. *"Respectable"* is the band returning to the Rave-Up way of doing things. Clapton is playing a Telecaster, which explains why his tone is different from what he would later develop. He still cuts through and you can easily hear his early mastery of the blues form, the fluid dexterity and why he stood out from the other guitar players. *"Five Long Years"*, *"Pretty Girl"* and *"Louise"* are songs that are obviously chosen because they don't fall into the category of: everyone else plays. Good songs, good performances and a good reaction from the audience.

Live Album Review

The Yardbirds are the real thing and play the music as if they are wise men that lived the tales they are signing about. They sound older than they actually are. "*I'm A Man*" is significantly different from "*Muddy Waters*". This rendition has a Yardbirds stamp on it with the speedy tempo and melodic changes. It works well, and it probably made little difference to the crowd, for most of them, in retrospect, never heard the original anyway.

"*Here Tis*" is another Rave-Up song. This one includes some call and response between the band as well as including the people in attendance. It sounds like the show stopping, end of the gig, leaving everything on the stage closer. That only makes the crowd want more. I'm sure there was more to this set than forty minutes. That was average for a vinyl album in 1964. America didn't get to hear it till later and that was when the Yardbirds were playing pop music. Clapton left for the group to release a single, "*For Your Love*", three months after this album was dropped. Changes needed to be made, and Clapton wasn't happy with them. John Mayall offered him the opportunity to explore his divinity, but with the Yardbirds, he was given the nick-name, "*Slow Hand.*" I didn't know it was because of how long he took to change a guitar string during a show. That, in itself, tells you that he didn't get rich playing in the Yardbirds. You would think he would have an extra guitar in the wings.

IT'S TOO LATE TO STOP NOW

BY: VAN MORRISON

IT'S TOO LATE TO STOP NOW is a much heralded and critically acclaimed double live album. It was released in 1974 and contains performances from shows in Los Angeles and London. What this album is not is a gratuitous, run-of-the-mill, greatest hits played live package. This is a stand-alone album that represents the emotionally intense and soulful voice of Van Morrison. This album defines what people, who have witnessed it, rave on about. What you get in concert is a totally different experience than what you get from the constrained, studio work.

He's backed by an eleven piece band, The Caledonia Soul Orchestra, that surrounds Van Morrison with magic, to allow him to get lost in the music, where his heart comes alive and flows out of his expressive and powerful vocals. He has always surrounded himself with incredible talent, who can put themselves into the songs they are fashioning. This creates a warm and organic environment where Van Mor-

Live Album Review

rison is trusting and comfortable to do "his thing" with restrained abandon.

There are eighteen songs on this set, drawn from previous albums, his days in the group Them and interpretations of American rhythm and blues. To list and glorify each one is not necessary. Van's muse touches everyone differently, so what I'm hearing and taking away from this will not be the same for anyone else. I can state that each listen will reveal something new, be it a blues groove, a mystical excursion or a nostalgic journey; it's an album that will draw you in and stay with you after the music's over. There's no hint of stardom and ego. It's a man who made an agreement with fame and recognition, to have the freedom to write songs and sing the songs he writes.

This album is a genuine article and honest and real as it gets. To purposely omit a performance of "*Moondance*" says all you need to know about Van Morrison because it's not about him anyway. When he ends the album with a shout to the crowd, "It's too late to stop now," it's a declaration of the calling on his life and the life he is bringing to it. That translates into what makes this live album one of the great ones: Passion.

LIVE! AT SUNBURY

BY: BILLY THORPE AND THE AZTECS

The only thing I remember from Billy Thorpe was the song, *"Children of the Sun"*. He never broke through in the United States but was big in Australia. That's the setting of this 1972 album, *AZTECS LIVE AT SUNBURY.* Sunbury was a music festival from the Land Down Under and 1972 was the inaugural year. There are some great stories surrounding the festival itself that I won't bother with here, only to say it was heavy on loud rock music that Australian crowds enjoyed more than the so-called hippie music. That being the aim, Billy Thorpe and the Aztecs were a perfect match, for their set was nothing but loud, rock music.

This double album contains only eight songs. That may seem skimpy but after all is said and done, over an hour of non-stop, heavy duty boogie has transpired. *"C.C Rider"* and *"Be Bop a Lula"* are the opening pair that the Aztecs pin their badges on. Bruce Howard plays electric piano that sounds like it's pumped through a Marshall Stack, Paul Wheeler

Live Album Review

plays bass that's drowning in fuzz that you feel more than hear and Gil Matthews on drums rides the cymbals like he's trying to keep them from flying away.

Let's not forget Billy Thorpe who plays excellent guitar and whose singing voice is like many, many others in the hard rock game of the day. This guy has got the pipes, the skills and the guitar bravado to go to the next level. Hearing what he does on the extended guitar solo on "*Momma*" should have been broadcasted throughout the world. Why he didn't, may have something to do with, in his words, "acid, smoke and booze," that he tells the crowd of over 60,000, before playing the song, "*Most People I Know Think I'm Crazy*". The song itself isn't all that good, even with the harmony vocals, but when the band takes it into instrumental territory, where they jam over a repetitive riff, is when Billy Thorpe and the Aztecs become contenders.

This is the pattern of everything here. Imagine taking the best elements of the bands, Cactus, Deep Purple and Grand Funk and fashioning it into your own boogie. That's what's happening here but remembering the year is 1972, the noise is basic and heavy with vocals that sometimes blur the lines between Steve Marriott and early Rod the Mod Stewart. It's good music, played loud and designed to reach a large mass of listeners. I like that every song ends as if it was a major event that needed a thunderous conclusion. It's clear that the over-the-top showmanship is professional, as is the stagecraft of Billy Thorpe, who works the crowd by playing his guitar in all the right places, verbally communicating and singing with real command. This guy has been around the block a few times and on this day, he owns Sunbury Festival, no doubt about it.

"*Rock Me Baby*" name drops B.B. King but sounds nothing like the blues. It's not even close until the band slows the tempo and lowers the volume to include the crowd in some hand clapping and singing.

"*Time to Live*" combines the Deep Purple, massive wall of sound with the shrill vocals of Steve Marriott. I kid you not, and this is happening in 1972, in Australia before there ever was an AC/DC.

"*Jump Back*" is where Billy breaks out his harmonica, and like the guitar, that Aussie boy can play. Tenminutes come and go before you realize, Billy and the Aztecs have taken you to the top of their pyramid, where the end is near. Nobody is getting sacrificed today. In fact, the only blood is from the fingers of the musicians working so hard. No, you're at the summit for fifteen minutes where you enjoy the party of "*Ooh Poo Pa Doo*", and get to sing and clap your hands to the beat. When the smoke clears, after the fire is extinguished, all that is left is the hike down the steps to solid ground.

Live Album Review

This album, for the longest time, was hard to come by. It is well regarded in Australia and should have been the ship that took Billy Thorpe into international waters. Why is it only a question? He was good enough but maybe not original enough, but even so, it was the early 70s. Maybe he should have auditioned for AC/DC. He sings better than Bon and plays guitar better than Angus. Maybe he was too good.

Live Album Review

FULL HOUSE

BY: J. GEILS BAND

Some crowd noise opens this 1972 live album, *LIVE! FULL HOUSE*. I think there should have been a countdown from ten, because this band blasts off from the opening song, "*First I Look at the Purse*". It's all a party for thirty minutes after that. Recorded at The Cinderella Ballroom in Detroit, the J. Geils Band is an adrenaline shot to the heart. Peter Wolf's energy on stage would kill lesser men. Magic Dick on harmonica feeds off the current that's being generated and Seth Justman on keyboards adds hot sauce to the tasty dish being served up. When Peter Wolf says, "Take out your false teeth baby because I wanna suck on your gums," it's only a teaser of what lies ahead. He playfully coaxes Magic Dick before, the now classic, "*Whammer Jammer*". Fast talkin' Boston jive is the norm and the band seems to play the songs at this speed. "*Hard Driving Man*" is rock and roll with an attitude.

Stephen J. Bell's thunderous drums keep the speed-

Edward Milano

ty of ax wizards anyway. The rhythm section is in the pocket and is the glue that keeps the party thumping along. MTV's exposure to their videos made The Geils Band famous and I believe that it caused some of the band's magic to fade away. The humor stayed intact though, and that same humor is all over this album.

They know all about the "tuff timz" and instead of preaching answers from the stage or writing songs about it, they offered a good time to help you forget your troubles for a couple hours. And they appreciated the audience's love. In fact, I think they were rock and roll vampires, for they got stronger and better on stage as they fed off the people in the crowd. If you attended a J.Geils Band show and woke up the next day with mysterious holes in your neck, now you know why.

Live Album Review

BLOW OUT YOUR FACE

BY: J. GEILS BAND

Some bands should never release studio albums. The J. Geils Band is at their best on stage. *BLOW OUT YOUR FACE* is a great title to a great live album. Released in 1976, the band had figured out how to pace their live shows. Their previous live album, *FULL HOUSE*, the music is delivered so fast you don't have time to catch your breath. Here, Peter Wolf is given the chance to do his comedy routines and work the crowd into a frenzy. I would hate to think his rap before the song, *"Must Have Got Lost"* is what this album is best known for, but I think it may be true. You have to laugh at Rapudah the Beaudah.

This is white boy soul music. This is a double album of a party. I like that the band plays an extended jam while Peter Wolf is off stage doing who knows what. Magic Dick is a harp master, Seth Justman is the MVP on keys, J.Geils never was a guitar hero, but he didn't have to be. They perform what is necessary and avoid being intrusive. The music biz has plen-

Edward Milano

ing freight train on the tracks. I, personally, would like a visual demonstration of the Detroit Demolition dance that Peter Wolf describes from the stage. I have a sneaking suspicion the venue was rocking so hard that night it was falling apart. Smart to next play the slowed down blues of, "*Serves You Right to Suffer*". Magic Dick, Seth Justman and (yes) J. Geils all take turns playing solos. This band didn't do enough blues and from this performance, it's a crying shame. The T.V. Time-Out is over and the party is back in full swing with the back-to-back classics of, "*Cruisin' For a Love*" and "*Lookin' For a Love*". It's clear, from the extended ending, that the boys didn't want to bring the concert to a close.

This is one of those shows you wish you were at. 1972 was when the J.Geils Band were making a name for themselves. This release would be the first of three live albums in their long career. This one is heralded as being the best. It is certainly a stand-alone album that you listen to in its entirety, and not focus on one or two choice tracks. It rocks from the get -go and still rings in your ears after you put your false teeth back in. You're exhausted, and you didn't even expend any physical energy. That, my friends, is a great live album. Even the cover artwork is creatively fun- an exclamation point of sorts. Do those false teeth still fit?

Live Album Review

THE APOLLO THEATRE PRESENTS IN PERSON THE JAMES BROWN SHOW

BY: JAMES BROWN

Some albums become a part of history and *THE APOLLO THEATRE PRESENTS IN PERSON THE JAMES BROWN SHOW* is one of those.

Every album that's held in such high regard comes with a backstory.

James Brown asked his record label at the time, King Records, to release a live album of his incendiary stage show. The record label at the time, King Records, declined James Brown's request for a live album of his incendiary stage show, citing the obvious reason that without the visual of the performance, the recorded music wouldn't hold up. James Brown went ahead and financed this record on his own to prove a point that it would sell. Since its release, in 1963, it has received numerous accolades and awards from smart people who know what they're talking and writing about.

Robert Chistgau says it's one of the essential albums of the 60s-70s. He's a pretty smart guy, as are the members of The Library of Congress, who entered this album into The National Recording Legacy. The album is also in The Grammy Hall of Fame. I didn't know these prestigious places existed because I'm not that smart, but the writers and editors at Rolling Stone Magazine know they are and they have this album sitting at #55 in their list of 500 Greatest Albums. That's impressive and with those credentials, it has to be as good a listen as those classic live albums by The Allman Brothers, The Who and Humble Pie.

I'm not smart, so that excuses me from saying this James Brown live album is not as good as those other albums, but to compare is not fair for this is soul music. The others had soul, but the music rocked, while James Brown is doing some early, funky things, which is what makes this album more of a fun and interesting listen than it is one you keep in constant rotation.

The actual show was in 1962 and James Brown and his band, The Famous Flames, are tight, professional and well rehearsed. The music clocks in just over thirty minutes, so it's short, to the point, and doesn't contain any filler or dead spots. It hits fast, right after the introduction (which is a Chitlin Circuit hold-over) and doesn't stop moving until the last horn blast. It's been said the audience noise is more canned

Live Album Review

than authentic, but it doesn't matter either way, for it adds to the charm of the album. The people are clapping and screaming, right on cue, in the right places, but that's a tradition at The Apollo. They aren't booing, cursing, and throwing things at the performers to leave the stage, which is also a tradition.

The sound is traveling so quick, it's hard to grab onto anything memorable. James is doing his 'thang'. It's oldies but not recognizable goodies. It's 1962, so he may feel good, but he hasn't written it down yet. There are some precursors to the funk he would go on to blaze a trail with and, of course, the slow and simmering "for ladies only" performances. The best here is the medley where he runs through eleven songs in over six minutes. That's one incredible feat of engineering and talent with all the rhythm and tempo changes, the vocal gymnastics and the various horn runs that don't miss. This is an early example of the infamous James Brown, the band-leader, that would direct his band, as he was singing and dancing. If anyone messed up, he heard it and would fine or fire the guilty party. Take that Frank Zappa.

Yes, this is a good live album. Is it as great as it's been declared as being? I don't know I'm not that smart and am not listening with the same intention, objective or education as the brainiacs who get to make those calls as to what is bad, what is good and what is great. I do appreciate that

James Brown was keeping his art as real as he could and was taking a huge and expensive risk with this release. It worked out, which empowered him to continue doing it his way. He didn't go to the finishing schools, singing pop songs and dressing in a nonthreatening manner to cross over. He was a sex machine.

Live Album Review

LIVE! IN CONCERT

BY: JAMES GANG

JAMES GANG LIVE IN CONCERT from 1971 would be Joe Walsh's last with the band. You could tell he was out-growing the confines of a three piece unit, where he was an equal member, even though he was the talent. The other two were good, but what the heck? This is a classic album from a show at Carnegie Hall. I love the album cover of the three horses tied outside the venue. The back cover is pure Joe Walsh humor.

Anyway, this is a Joe Walsh album, pure and simple. He sings, plays electric and acoustic guitar and Hammond organ. The band is tight, and that comes from gigging, and rehearsing together for years. Joe just grew up, that's all. *"You're Gonna Need Me"*, *"Walk Away"*, and *"Lost Woman"* are the stand-outs. *"You're Gonna Need Me"* is a slow blues that shows Joe's all-around abilities as a guitarist. *"Walk Away"* is heavy metal. Man, does that bass roar. *"Lost Woman"* is a Yardbirds' cover and the band all take turns showing off their chops.

In the late 60s to the mid 70s, British rock bands were arrogant, thinking all the great rock guitarists were from their little island. They claimed credit for Hendrix and Duane Allman had to die to get noticed. Joe Walsh's guitar playing, on the other hand, was respected by everyone. Pete Townsend raved over him, as did Steve Marriott and Jeff Beck. This live set shows why. Sure, the band comes off in places like a poor man's Cream, but Joe Walsh comes off as the young guitar player from America that people should pay attention to. Guess what? They did.

Live Album Review

Edward Milano

LIVE!

BY: THE EAGLES

Okay. It's 1980 and the most successful band of the 1970s has disbanded because you're an a-hole. Problem was that your record company wanted the two albums your band still owes them. Easy fix -give them a double live album. Problem was you can't do anything unless the other a-hole in the band approves. Another easy fix: work on opposite sides of the country. I'm not trying to be funny. That's how ridiculous it got between Henley and Frey. *LIVE!* has to be the most heavily overdubbed live album in the history of live albums. What does it matter? Eagle fans just want a prod- uct. They'll give them a pass. Now, the majority of Eagle fans were females who liked the country flavor and dudes that played in cover bands. Every bar band played "*Peaceful Easy Feeling*". That's a fact and in fact, this whole album gets a pass.

Why the band never released live albums from the previous incarnations is anyone's guess. Pass. What's actual live performance and what's studio tweaking? Who knows? Pass. *"Hotel California"* is good. *"Life in the Fast Lane"* is good. *"Heartache Tonight"* is good too. All the performances are good, except for *"New Kid in Town"* but that's because I hate that song. This is The Eagles. Henley and Frey weren't going to put out any garbage. I admire the desire for quality but it got to be such an obsession, it broke the band up. I would have preferred to hear them without any overdubs. Joe Walsh and Don Felder's guitars mesh well. I'm not sure why they included a solo tune of Joe's. I mean *"Life's Been Good"* is alright, but why bypass excellent Eagle material for that? Pass. I'm glad they didn't pass up the chance to give Randy some love and included some performances from 1976, but why include *"Doolin' Dalton II?"* Pass. I am happy they let that hippie, Timothy, have a song on here. He has such a sweet voice. It makes you want to pass out. No wonder Poco grabbed him to fill Randy's shoes when he quit them to form The Eagles.

When Randy quit The Eagles, guess who quit Poco? Timmy would not pass on the opportunity to join The Eagles. The vinyl even has messages scrawled into the out grooves on both sides of each disc. My favorite one is, *"I've gotta rest up for my monster"*. For me, the best track on this album is, *"Seven Bridges Road"*. It's five-part, a Capella harmony sounds really, really cool, man. How much of it is actually live, I don't know. Pass. It was pretty smart to include that unre-

Live Album Review

leased track. It boosted sales. Nobody ever claimed Henley and Frey were stupid.

The musical credits sure, include a cast of many. I don't recall that many people on stage. I do know Joe Vitale played some drums, so give out another pass. Who cares? It's The Eagles. They can do anything they want.

Edward Milano

RAUNCH AND ROLL LIVE

BY: BLACK OAK ARKANSAS

I forgot I even had this album. Talk about ahead of their time. These guys were as redneck as it comes and it was no act. They would have had a reality show if they were around today. I'm not even sure if they were considered a southern rock band. I don't think they were even given the chance to pledge into the fraternity. This live album is from 1973 and the title pretty much defines what's inside. I remember at age fifteen, I was arguing with a neighbor, who was a few years older than me, which in his mind, meant he knew more than me. In fact, I think he thought he knew everything, probably still does. Anyway, how we got into a discussion of Black Oak Arkansas I don't remember, but I do remember him stating, "They are just no good." Despite my attempts at pointing out the intellectual complexities of their art, he would not budge from his position. So I will review this live album, *RAUNCH AND ROLL LIVE* from the 'no good' band.

It's music from the Ozarks, home of Jed, Jethro and

Live Album Review

Granny.

The music is raw. What holds it together is the superb drumming of Tommy Aldridge, who would later drum for almost everyone in rock. If anything good came from this band, it was him but getting back to the album. The cover is downright creepy. The silver things on Jim Dandy's fingers are thimbles. He used them for playing the washboard and he does a credible job on the song, "*When Electricity Came to Arkansas*". That is one of the more interesting songs on the set. The others are rock and roll or, better yet, raunch and roll.

Imagine a trio of guitarists that all suck. Imagine the Three Stooges with guitars. The three guitarists in this band can't even sound like one good guitarist. I enjoyed listening to the solos on the final song, "*Up*" which is supposed to be the climatic, jamming, guitar hero, finish to their set. It's over nine minutes long and that's nine minutes of my life, I'll never get back. The only standout track is "*Mutants of The Monster*". It's a protest song like "*My Generation*" by The Who. It's not bad, really, and would be excellent if someone else did it. I'm sorry but Jim Dandy Mangrum cannot sing. Keith Richards and Bob Dylan on their bad days still sound better. I could never tell if that gravel voice was real or fake. It sounds like some old man after a life of moonshine and chaw.

Am I giving you the impression I dislike this record?

Edward Milano

I Love this record. I love it because it's real. Punk rock can't even touch it. Grunge bands with all their flannel and liberal eco-integrity can't touch it. Black Oak meant business. You can tell by the performances here they were serious and I applaud them for it. You can't argue with something simple, loud and erratic. It's a heaping helping of good times. Besides, if it wasn't for Jim Dandy, there would be no Diamond David Lee Roth. That's meant to be complimentary. Diamond Dave stole everything from Jim Dandy's stage persona. The tight pants, the bare chest, the long blond hair, the jumps, the kicks, the sword-play, the scarves and the sexual bravado. Songs from this album, *"Gettin' Kinda Cocky"*, *"Gigolo"*, *"Hot Rod"* , and *"Hot And Nasty"* would fit as song titles on any Van Halen album from the David Lee Roth era. When it came to rock songs about sex, Ted Nugent was a hunter and gatherer, Frank Zappa was a sociologist and AC/DC was a formula.

Give some love to Black Oak Arkansas. They were lovers of all things women and appreciated the beauty and power they had over men. I'm sure fellow Arkansas boy, Bill Clinton, were influenced by their machismo too. If more people knew about Black Oak, then they would understand Slick Willie and his appetites. *"Slick Willie."* Now that would make a great song title since *"Devil in a Blue Dress"* was already taken.

LIVE! AT WOODSTOCK

BY: CREEDENCE CLEARWATER REVIVAL

Fifty years is a long time. *LIVE! AT WOODSTOCK* is an archival release that, for no real good reason, was hidden away, as if it never happened. John Fogerty insisted the band's lackluster performance not be included in the Woodstock movie and subsequent albums. This turned out to be just another bad business decision, which resulted in many people not even knowing CCR was at Woodstock, much less a headliner. I have my theories about John Fogerty's refusal, but after listening to this album, fifty years after the fact, I know it wasn't due to the music.

They kick things off with *"Born On the Bayou"* and *"Green River"*. The sound quality is great and John Fogerty is singing strong as he attacks his guitar. Stu Cook on bass, Doug Clifford on drums and brother Tom Fogerty on guitar serve as a tight, rhythm section that gives John space to sing the songs and play lead guitar. I still feel this ensemble created the right mood for the "swamp rock" that John Fogerty was going for. He has since used other musicians to back him on the stage, but nobody did it better than Stu, Doug and Tom. I don't care what John says about their lack of skill. It's rock and roll and it's more about feel than flash.

The set list follows with "*Ninety-Nine*" and a "*Half Won't Do*" where the band tried their hand at R&B while John sings like a soul man. He has the voice to pull it off but not the experiences to sell it. It still is the only official, live CCR performance of this tune, so that makes it a keeper. That also goes for the run through of "*Bootleg*". John counts it off fast, after complaining about the monitors, but everyone nails it with little problem.

The next three of "*Commotion*", "*Bad Moon Rising*" and "*Proud Mary*" are played in similar and spirited, gratuitous fashion. They are quick, they are close to the studio versions and they are recognized by the crowd, who seem to come alive by cheering at their conclusions.

There is little banter from the stage, with an occasional pause between songs, to fix something. When John does address the crowd, it's barely audible.

I think the last four songs are the strongest of the complete show. Maybe the band is warmed up and reality is setting in to the cultural significance of this event. It's clear that John is confident and is making every effort to do his best.

Live Album Review

"I Put A Spell On You" is sinister. John's howling and the band's locked-in steady groove create a sinister atmosphere.

"The Night Time is the Right Time" brings back some bluesy soul that sets up the one-man jam session that is to follow.

"Keep On Chooglin" is over ten minutes of John wailing on his harmonica. This became a standard of CCR shows and this version is basically the same as on *THE CONCERT* and *EUROPE* live sets.

"Suzie Q" runs close to eleven minutes and features John and his improvisational skills on lead guitar. He's no Jimi Hendrix, Carlos Santana or Alvin Lee (celebrated from their appearances in the movie) but he doesn't have to be. Their musical style was original and what John Fogerty does is perfect for CCR's sound. The crowd cheers loudly at the finale, which tells me that John's view that everyone was asleep in the mud when the band went on at midnight is revisionist history and a poor excuse for not allowing anything to be documented.

I really think John Fogerty just had a poor attitude, simple as that. The Grateful Dead played before CCR that day, and their set ran a little long to John's liking. It's The Dead, and John knew full-well that was common, not to mention it rained like crazy that day, which all but wrecked the schedule.

Others in the San Francisco scene never accepted and respected CCR, based in Oakland, according to John's feelings. That probably had more to do with his decision, since there were many of those perceived snobs at Woodstock. He went on stage that night with an ax to grind and his memory of one guy, on a hill, holding a light, as the only person awake during their set, is wrong. John, without question, felt bad about CCR collecting the fattest check of all the artists at Woodstock, for an hour's work. His band played so badly that he probably gave the money back. He would have been better off smoking some good herb instead of playing it sober. He might have relaxed and, as a joke, opened the show with "*Midnight Special*".

Regardless of what shakes out, this is a good concert from a band that was just hitting its stride. *GREEN RIVER* was just released and *WILLIE AND THE POOR BOYS* and *COSMOS FACTORY* were to follow. The original Woodstock movie and album would only have helped their trajectory. I could just see, in the movie, John singing, "barefoot girl dancing in the moonlight" as the camera pans to some hippie chick, swaying to the music. I know the anniversary editions and expanded releases of Woodstock featured some CCR, but if anything, this album only fuels criticism against

Live Album Review

John Fogerty, which makes me wonder why they released it at all. The name of Fantasy on the label is probably the reason.

GRAND FUNK LIVE!

BY: GRAND FUNK

In 1970, Grand Funk Railroad was on fire. Hated by the critics and ignored by the radio, they still sold millions of records and toured relentlessly. Terry Knight, the Svengali slave driving manager, almost killed these guys. This album is a true, 'as if you were there' experience. You either loved or hated this. It's raw energy. I think they rushed this out there because of the band's popularity, but who cares what I think anyway?

"*Are You Ready*" opens the show, and the band doesn't let up till the show is over. "*Paranoid*" (not the Black Sabbath song) is next, and you can tell the band has developed their chops from the sloppy studio version they released. Some say that Grand Funk are lousy musicians. I disagree. Don Brewer is the most underrated drummer in rock. Frank Zappa offered him a job, and Frank didn't employ 'lousy' musicians. Mel Schancher's bass work is in your face, and as metal as Geezer Butler. Mark Farner is adequate as a guitarist. I always felt this band would have been better with a lead

Live Album Review

guitarist and Mark handling rhythm duties. I suppose if they were a punk rock band, the musicianship would never have been an issue, for we all know how gifted The Sex Pistols and The Clash were. When the boys do "Inside Looking Out". It is the best version of this song ever and I don't care how good your crummy band played it.

GFR is passionate and your crummy band played it to get chicks. Mark changes the lyric of "burlap bag" to "nickel bag" which makes him cool. He was also taking a stance against hard drugs as evidenced by his speech before he performed, *"Mean Mistreater"* on the electric piano. I'm not sure how the drug dealers in the crowd felt about it.

Like 'em or not, Grand Funk had good concert material, which are songs designed to be played as loud as possible with heavy distortion. *"Heartbreaker"*, *"In Need"* and *"T.N.U.C"* all come off well. The band jams some and gets the crowd going on 'Mark Says Alright!' before ending with a long version of their pre-*"Closer To Home"* epic- *"Into The Sun"*. There isn't a rock band, now or then, that wouldn't want some of Grand Funk's songs as their own. I say that with all sincerity.

People thought that the Atlanta International Pop Festival was the site where this double album was recorded. They actually recorded the double album at gigs in Florida. They took the cover photograph in Atlanta. To be honest, I'm sure the music sounded the same.

Edward Milano

Live Album Review

LIVE! AFTER DEATH

BY: IRON MAIDEN

Bow and pay tribute to the godz of metal. *LIVE! AFTER DEATH*, from 1985, has received enough acclaim and accolades that it's become a subject of contention. I agree with its greatness, but if it belongs in the hallowed halls of rock immortality, it needs to be placed in a section devoted to the 1980s. Hard Rock and Metal music in the 70s was a different beast. Much of it was created by mad scientists that had no clue what they were doing and made it up, as they were going along. What was created and produced during that era influenced and shaped what came after. Iron Maiden came after and they came with a master plan and a blueprint because they (or Steve Harris) had a clue and knew what they were doing.

There's so much I can and want to say about the legacy of this band, the music and their buddy, Eddie but I'll just cut to the chase. *LIVE! AFTER DEATH* is a great live album and a double, at that. I think, because it was either vinyl or cassette, that it was one of the last of its kind. Call it a blaze of glory. Great songs? All of them. The band has said there were no overdubs. Good. It's real and it's really good.

If you were, or still are, into this band then you know all about the attack of Iron Maiden. Bruce Dickenson's vocals, Dave Murray and Adrian Smith's dual guitar play, Steve Harris' bass work, which is the foundation for the band's sound and Nicko McBrian, whose kick took metal to the next level. This album keeps badass company with the other classic live albums that are too good to review. They exist and are as great today, as they were yesterday, and will continue to be in the future. This one doesn't need any further kudos, just an exhumation of the sarcophagus.

Iron Maiden got some heat for their image, some songs and for the mascot. They knew what they were doing with the album cover art and the sinister titles. Horror movies were huge in the 1980s and that crossed over into all facets of the entertainment industry. WWF used Iron Maiden songs and Michael Jackson's *"Thriller"* would have been better if he had Iron Maiden playing on it. It was so obvious and I was amazed they got any flack at all. The controversy helped them, but did they have to go that route? Leave that stuff to Madonna. This band was more about history and literature. Parents and teachers should have been happy the kids were being exposed to it. That evil band wrote and performed

Live Album Review

complex songs about The Battle of Britain, The Charge of the Light Brigade, Outlaws of the Old West, The Book of Revelation, Native American Indians, The Tower of London, need I go on? They should have given the critics a piece of their mind and some of this should have been required listening in school. Schoolhouse Rock got nothing on this.

My list of songs from this album that never get old are: "*The Trooper.*" Only one? No, I like every one of them (seventeen if you're counting). I singled out "*The Trooper*" because there isn't a better song to head pound and play air guitar to, no matter how old you are, especially if nobody is around to see you do it. Every song on LIVE AFTER DEATH is sharp as a sword and accurate as a powder musket. Imagine what it was like to be, up the irons, at one of their concerts, experiencing the surround sound effects of being in the cockpit of a WWII Spitfire. Many fables can be told. This is not IMAX. Woe to you, for it is Iron Maiden. Iron Maiden guaranteed the quality assurance because they had the right group of musicians who were at the top of their game. Martin Birch may have had a thing or two to assist in the merriment. This corporation did fine and who am I to question the direction or business acumen? Yes, Eddie is a corporate puppet and Iron Maiden is a trademark. I like it better when the product of music is good. You can keep Eddie. Don't meddle with things you don't understand.

BURSTING OUT

BY: JETHRO TALL

Released in 1978, *BURSTING OUT*, by Jethro Tull, would be a 'last hurrah' for this line-up. Ian Anderson, Martin Barre, John Evan, Barrriemore Barlow, David Palmer and John Glascock were a long-standing band and in some circles of Tull fans, the best at bringing Ian Anderson's visions to life. As far as live albums go, this is a complete show. Ian is credited as the producer and it wouldn't be beyond his desires to fix mistakes in the studio, but this gives off an authentic sound. Very few early Jethro Tull songs make the cut.

It opens with *"No Lullaby"* (a current tune at the time) followed by *"Sweet Dream"* from way back. Two decent songs, but there were many, many great Tull songs available to play than those. Disappointing, if you're a Tull fan, but their average songs are better than most bands' great songs. Jethro Tull was in a stage of transition and the next three selections were where Ian Anderson was going, artistically. The band played *"Skating Away"*, *"Jack In The Green"* and *"One*

Live Album Review

Brown Mouse" acoustically. It works, but they rush through them, giving the listener little chance to appreciate the performances. In fact, the band seems to play everything faster than necessary, as if they want to cram as much music into a small window of allotted time. This band is so good, they are painting this concert by numbers.

Ian Anderson had a reputation of being a hard taskmaster but here he's having fun and seems resigned to the fact that the large arena audience couldn't care less how pristine the music is. They want the good Tull songs and Ian Anderson delivers some of them. "*Thick As A Brick*" and "*Minstrel In The Gallery*" is a 'Cliff Notes' version, but it's more than enough. How does a poet and writer of complicated musical passages make it work for a large crowd? Ian Anderson figured it out. Keep it simple and dumb it down. His trademark flute is ever present, as well as his acoustic guitar. He is the show! He interacts with his audience as a stand-up comedian, and probably would have had a career as one had he not chosen music.

His band are pieces to his jigsaw puzzle and each plays a character. Ian breaks out a great flute solo and improvisation before the band joins in on "*God Rest Ye Merry Gentlemen/Bouree*". I'm certain he stood on one leg during this, but from the pictures provided, no codpiece. This was before computers, so I still wonder how Ian replicates the harmony voices on *"Songs From The Wood"*. Still, it's a credible performance, considering the studio version was some great progressive music. Jethro Tull sets the crowd up for what they came for.

"Hunting Girl" is a great rocker, and it features the guitar wizardry of Martin Barre Whom in my opinion, is one of the greatest rock guitarists from the 70s. He seems like a man void of ego and okay with playing in the shadow of Ian Anderson for his career and I'm sure it was the right choice. Remember, he replaced Tony Iommi. Let's skip the filler stuff, like *"Too Old To Rock and Roll"* and the excellent drum solo from Barriemore Barlow on *"Conundrum"*. Let's get to the stuff the masses yearn for.

The Warhorses are let out of the stable. It's Ian Anderson, playing the songs that made him semi-famous, and ones he would choose to forget, if he could. *"Cross-Eyed Mary"* starts the parade, with Ian's nasty flute and John Evan's piano chords. The crowd cheers. Oh, yeah....

Kick out the Zeps. Ian Anderson had a mutual dislike for Led Zep, which was never explained. Here he shows he and his band can do anything they can with better lyrics. This band rocks hard with the little progressive, complicated stuff. It's meat and potatoes with a touch of the blues. *"Aqualung"* and *"Locomotive Breath"* follow a short, hard rock, Irish jig with *"Quatrain"*, sandwiched between. John Evan gets to

Live Album Review

throw in some classical piano improvisation and the chords of LB bring the crowd to a crescendo. This is Jethro Tull playing wild and crazy music. No gentlemanly restraints of proper, upper class pretension here. This is rock and roll at its finest.

They bring the crowd down by finishing with a pomp-ous instrumental, "*The Dambusters March*". A sad farewell of sorts, for this group of musicians would never play as a unit again. They were good and this live album, *BURSTING OUT*, is good as well. After this, Jethro Tull began its decline. Ian Anderson tried to reinvent himself, which is a shame be-cause he was such an original. To stay relevant, with his trusty companion, Martin Barre, Ian would still make music into the 80s, some awash in synths and some sounding like Dire Straits. Hey, Jethro Tull won a Grammy for Hard Rock/Metal over Metallica. There's some accounting for good taste.

U.S.A

BY: KING CRIMSON

King Crimson, or should I say, Robert Fripp, released USA, as a concluding benediction to the band and its fan base. The band, at this time, comprised: John Wetton on bass and vocals, Bill Bruford on drums and percussion, David Cross on violin and mellotron, and that friend of the devil himself, Robert Fripp (someone should do a study on that guy) on guitar and mellotron. I'm not sure why Satan was such a popular theme in rock music in the 70s, but Scratch is all over this album. If the name of your band is King Crimson, then why ask why?

If you're brave enough to listen to this album, I suggest you take a valium beforehand, because the intense music might compel you to go outside and destroy stuff. The instrumentals of "*Larks Tongue in Aspic*" and "*Asbury Park*" are industrial strength, Drano. They are relentless chaos with brief snippets of space to breathe. It's like being inside the mind of a serial killer. The violin is a nice touch, for it takes the

Live Album Review

edge off the sonic violence, but the effect is more like Nero fiddling while Rome is burning.

John Wetton sang *"Easy Money"*, *"Lament"* and"Exile", his voice is similar to the previous guy that joined ELP, only more aggressive and venomous. In fact, the whole parade here is aggressive and venomous. The band is flawless in their execution and Fripp's guitar playing is best described as calculated. If one is familiar and appreciative of his unique approach, then you will love him on this. There are some moments of calm and beauty, only to have it suddenly destroyed by a crashing tidal wave.

"20th Century Schizoid Man" ends this onslaught and thank you, Jesus. King Crimson is cumbersome and you wonder if they can pull it off. It's a ruse. They nail this one to the floor. The band nails the complicated time signatures and volume control, performing them to perfection and creating a frantic atmosphere. The vocals are so painfully distorted, they are abrasive. Don't play it too loud or the paint will peel off the walls. If you like the sound of fingernails on a chalkboard, then this is your English cup of tea.

Fripp would put in the liner notes of this album RIP. Too bad this band was excellent and the noise they created live is progressive, heavy metal brilliance. A more fitting description would be 'Jazz from Hell'.

LIVE! RUST

BY: NEIL YOUNG

LIVE RUST is Neil Young and Crazy Horse in all their ragged glory. Released in 1979, just four months after the career altering, *RUST NEVER SLEEPS*, this live set is Mister Young celebrating his 70s hippie sentiments while cleverly blasting into the 80s with a new look and expanded world-view.

I can only make an educated guess as to why they released this so hastily after a studio album that was still performing well on the charts. It even includes four songs from *RUST NEVER SLEEPS*. In fact, since most of that studio album was pulled from performances on the 1978 tour (that this live album is from), the four tunes are similar sounding. It doesn't matter one bit and if possible, the four-sided vinyl LP is the best way to be impacted, but any auditory delivery system is still acceptable.

The album begins with Shakey doing a solo spot on *"Sugar Mountain"*, *"I Am A Child"*, *"Comes A Time"* and *"After*

Live Album Review

The Gold Rush". He instantly connects with the crowd (and listener) by covering some spaces during his productive decade of the 70s, by singing, picking his guitar and playing harmonica on some great and recognizable tunes. It's when he includes "*My My, Hey Hey*" (out of the blue), then it all makes sense. This would have been a new song to the audience and although fits well with Neil's past acoustic songs, it has an edge, far from mellow. Neil attacks the guitar strings and delivers the vocals in a manner close to shouting. Elvis and Johnny Rotten both get a mention and you can feel the tension as he introspectively sings about an industry that eats its young.

Neil is up to something and when he brings Crazy Horse out to play two quick tunes, "*When You Dance*" and "*The Loner*". you have to wonder what. It's been said that Neil sounds best when he's backed by Crazy Horse and I agree, providing they have the right material.

This evening, they are without a doubt, "The Third Best Band In The World." The two songs are short and in the past, Neil used them as a vehicle to explore but he instead settled the band into "*The Needle And The Damage Done*" and "*Lotta Love*". Time is fading away quickly and these songs are nothing but the eye of a hurricane and during the performances, I can visualize the roadies dressed as Jawas running around on stage, in front of the oversized amplifier props, fixing the gear so the band can blow the roof off the place. Why the recording of the "*No Rain*" the chant from Woodstock is there is a mystery and I'll just let that sail away.

"*Sedan Delivery*" is a remarkable change of style and was Neil Young's statement to the punk rockers of the late 70s. That he 'ain't a dinosaur' and along with Crazy Horse couldn't forget as much as those 'kids' would ever know.. "*Powderfinger*", "*Cortez The Killer*", and "*Cinnamon Girl*" follow this onslaught of energy.

"*Powderfinger*" is a new one that would end up on *RUST NEVER SLEEPS* and it's played in the same fashion with some guitar feedback at the end that Neil is experimenting with that he would perfect on his live album, *WELD*. "*Cortez The Killer*" breaks into a reggae chant of, "he come dancin' across the water mon." which would be funny if the song's subject wasn't so serious. It's a great take of the song and close but different from the original. "*Cinnamon Girl*" is short and over just as you, as a listener, start to groove. This is another one of those older, endless jam songs that wind up condensed. Bummer man, but all is right when Young, Molina, Talbot, and Samedro sweep into "*Hurricane*". As expected, the 'Horse' provides that special ingredient that serves Neil like no other. I don't think anyone has been able to figure it out so long may they run. He is doing things with his guitar, with effects and harmonics. He hasn't done that before

Live Album Review

and it's a grand display of Neil, at his best, when he is lost in space.

"*Hey Hey, My My (Into The Black)*" , the now familiar, rocking companion piece to the acoustic one, is so distorted it sounds like the band is throwing sonic, razor blades at the audience. The closing song of 'Tonight's The Night' is probably the best version of it and is not even close to the quaalude insomnia from the original studio album. Neil and company sing the chorus in tight harmony before they get funky and downright nasty. This updated take would go on to become a concert staple and here is the first glimpse of how Neil Young beat the punks, the industry and those who thought his star had faded, when It was only just rising. Looking back, it seems he had a crystal ball and could see what direction the world and the fickle music scene was going and he was going to exist there on the fringes. There were new causes to confront and he was motivated, primed and ready to roll.

Comes A Time indeed. This album is another one of a long list where Neil would surface with nonconformity and a cache of amazing music. Instead of being a has-been, he now had the 80s to look forward to, with shorter hair.

Edward Milano

Live Album Review

STRANGER IN THIS TOWN

BY: MICK TAYLOR

If Mick Taylor had released this album after he left The Rolling Stones, instead of in 1990, his career would have taken a more lucrative route. This is a blues album, and it's recorded live in Sweden.

The opening tune, which is the only rock and roll type number and the namesake of the album, "*Stranger In This Town*". Would have been a great Stones song had Keef and Mick let him do more than just play tasty guitar. His singing voice is surprisingly good. Not great, but better than Keith Richards or Ronnie Wood.

Why do I keep interjecting The Rolling Stones in this review? Because I feel their best period musically was when Mick Taylor was in the band. Enuff said. Some Stones songs make it here: "*You Gotta Move*", "*Little Red Rooster*" and "Jumping Jack Flash". Taylor states in the liner notes that JJF is his favorite song of theirs. Class act. No steely knives or bad blood here. Mick Taylor has class, and that's what this album oozes. With musicians like Max Middleton and Eric Parker behind him, the music is top shelf. No bum notes, nothing overcooked, no showboating... It's Mick Taylor demonstrating why he has such a great reputation as a guitar players' guitarist. His rendition of "*Red House*" intertwined with "*Goin' Down Slow*" is a tribute to Hendrix, but he plays it nothing like Hendrix. He plays like Mick Taylor, which makes it all the more enjoyable. The song that puts the exclamation point on this whole album is "*Goin' South*". It's over ten minutes of joy that would make Carlos Santana proud.

Harkening back to Taylor's contributions to the Stones, you can hear glimpses of, "*Can You Hear Me Knocking?*" It's no wonder the band was upset when he decided to hand in his resignation. Anyway, good luck finding this gem because it's out of print, but for the right price I'm sure it can be had.

Live Album Review

HOT AUGUST NIGHT

BY: NEIL DIAMOND

HOT AUGUST NIGHT is an iconic, double live album that was studied by other artists and their management as the blueprint for changing a career overnight. Packaging, musical selection, promotion and distribution were all factors and many students like Peter Frampton, Kiss and Bob Seger aced their exams. Some students didn't test very well (David Bowie-*DAVID LIVE*) but there's no shame in trying and one can always take the exam again.

In August 1972, Neil Diamond was playing a ten, sold-out show residency at the outdoor Greek Theatre in Los Angeles. I'm sure the title is making reference to both the temperature and Mister Diamond's performance from August 24th. At this moment in time, he was making a serious attempt to go from just another writer and singer of Top 40 pop songs to an adult contemporary star. This live album was a good move, and the follow-up studio album, *MOODS*, all but cemented the transition.

Edward Milano

The album cover is still a mystery to me. What is he doing and what is it supposed to mean? The picture on the back is pretty cool. The backlit stage shows Neil's silhouette in all his long-haired glory, guitar strapped on and one arm raised to the sky with a peace symbol salute. That's more of a rock star pose. If you didn't know it was Neil Diamond you may think it was.....dare I say, Bon Jovi.

Musically, this album was right on time. A band of studio pros and an orchestra backs Neil.. The musical director and Neil allow the band to add their own embellishments. They stay within the confines of each song, but careful listening reveals there's some nice stuff happening underneath Neil's singing.

The songs are close to the originals, but different enough to make them more exciting. He's in a wonderful voice and provides many hits on this hot night: "*Solitary Man*", "*Cherry Cherry*", "*Sweet Caroline*", "*Play Me*", "*Song Sung Blue*", "*Cracklin Rosie*", "*Red Red Wine*", "*Shilo*", "*Girl You'll Be A Woman Soon*", "*I am I Said*" and "*Brother Love's Traveling Salvation Show*". Whew... that doesn't include the less popular, but still good, "*Crunchy Granola Suite*", "Canta Libre", "*Soolamin*" and "*Done Too Soon*". There's also some silly fodder with "*Porcupine Pie*" and "*Soggy Pretzels*". It would have been fun if Neil would have included some of his songs that were hits for other people but why bother. He

Live Album Review

has enough stuff of his own to make it a well-rounded show, paced just right. With just enough stage banter to keep everyone interested and to let you know Neil cares and plays for each individual person in attendance. Including the freeloading, "tree people." If he's rocking out, being silly, sweetly singing or just a man and his guitar, communicating with his crowd, he is hot. When he gets to the concluding *"Brother Love's Traveling Salvation Show"* he is uplifting and evangelical..

Hot can also be a fitting description for his sexual bravado. I won't name names or list song titles, but some of the lyrics reveal Neil has some issues. Is he sexually frustrated, a dirty old man, a pervert or just humorously trying to beat the censors at their own game? I don't know, but I think it's funny I never picked up on that side of Neil Diamond's art. Maybe a young Chaim Witz, at this time, was taking notes. If so, he cashed in on more than just the live album idea.

RAINBOW ON STAGE

BY: RAINBOW

RAINBOW ON STAGE is Ritchie's Blackmore and his musical vision in 1977. Recorded mostly in Europe, where the band was building a decent fan base, this album is all about Ritchie Blackmore. He, of course, had Ronnie James Dio, who brought the Dungeons and Dragons' theme to the songs and was still learning his craft. Blackmore dumped the amateurs of ELF, who recorded the 1st Rainbow album and surrounded himself with Tony Carey, Jimmy Bain and Cozy Powell. What a band. Just looking at the pic on the cover, it's clear the stage show had colorful lights, a huge rainbow and lots of fog. Very Spinal Tap.

The opening number is *"Kill The King"* which sounds very similar to *"Mob Rules"* when Sabbath later employed Dio's services. *"Man On The Silver Mountain"* follows, which is a borrowed riff from Deep Purple's *"Sail Away"*. The most interesting tune from the opening barrage is called *"Blues"*. It's nothing more than Blackmore and Carey trading blues

Live Album Review

licks and echoing each other over a basic 12-bar blues backing. Blackmore did this during his 'Purple days' with Ian Gillan. Only Tony Cary used his keyboards and coaxed some pretty interesting sounds.

Dio finishes this off by singing thirty seconds of the hit single "*Starstruck*". He completes this journey by singing to everyone that they in the crowd are indeed "*The Man On The Silver Mountain*" I feel so disappointed that I wasn't there that night because it's every boy's secret dream to be 'The Man On The Silver Mountain'. What makes this live set is the two long numbers; "*Catch The Rainbow*" and "*Mistreated*". Both are basically showcases for Ritchie Blackmore's guitar work. Always, self loathing and jaded that he never received the recognition his peers did. Mainly Page, Beck and Clapton. Blackmore left the security of Deep Purple to find that recognition. On the song, "Catch The Rainbow" beautifully sung by Dio, it's over fifteen minutes of Blackmore pulling out every trick in his bag of guitar magic. Color, shade, dynamics, bombast, light and dark.It's effect pedal heaven and yes, he is excellent.

He outpaces Jimmy Page. The only problem is Jimmy Page already did it. On "*Mistreated*" a Deep Purple song, not sung well by Dio (It's Coverdale's song). Blackmore tries to show everyone he can bend notes. That he makes the guitar sing better than Beck and can lay down some funky blues licks better than Clapton. Again, it's been done before. Besides, "*Mistreated*" is not that good of a song in the first place to devote 13 minutes of your set to it. The album ends with "*Still I'm Sad*" an old Yardbirds tune. When the band thanked everyone in the crowd, obviously German, they started chanting in unison, "UTA RAINBOW!"

Over and over it goes on. It sounds as if they were starting a riot.I don't think the Rainbow crowd was angry, or maybe they were because they were expecting more Deep Purple songs.

LIVE!

BY: ROBIN TROWER

If you can tell people that Robert Fripp took guitar lessons from you then you can boast about your abilities as a guitar player. Robin Trower never did. Nor did he ever complain about his being overlooked as one of the greatest guitar players in the rock era. He is a true gentleman and a phenomenal guitarist. He showed Mr. Fripp how to make a guitar "bend and wobble" and on this album, he's showing us what that sounds like.

This album was recorded in 1975, and Robin Trower was making some noise. His album *BRIDGE OF SIGHS* was popular, and three selections from that album are here. Of course the ones you would expect. *"Bridge of Sighs"* and *"Day Of The Eagle"* are missing, which at the time of this release in 1976, disappointed many fans.

"Too Rolling Stoned" opens the festivities, and it's all good from there. The song, *"Daydream"* is a beautiful performance that only gets better with each listen. *"Rock Me Baby"*

is all James Dewar, who was and will always be one of the finest electric blues singers. I could go on about each individual track it's all so good.

Robin Trower is a master. His work on the Strat (some have claimed he was channeling Hendrix) is without peer. This is an example of a player becoming one with his instrument. The emotion he pulls out is from his soul, which probably explains why he always looks in pain when he plays. Some might say, after listening to a song or two, that it doesn't sound all that difficult. Just try it. Trower was a master of his floor pedals and as you hear his work on this set, it sounds seamless. I have heard others, both live and on record play *"Day of the Eagle"*. Sure, you can play the song, but you can't make it sound like Robin Trower. Nobody can. That is what makes this live album so special. Add James Dewar's singing and Bill Lordans' drums that are "raggedy clean and sloppy tight," you have music that's often imitated but never duplicated.

Live Album Review

Edward Milano

239

Live Album Review

ALOHA FROM HAWAII

BY: ELVIS PRESLEY

Taking on this album feels like a walk on hallowed ground. My friends, when informed of this undertaking, advised me to avoid anything related to "The King." It can only end badly.

A glutton for a punishment, I put on a utility belt, my cape, wrapped a scarf around my neck, and packed a jar of Skippy for tribute. Then wore dark sunglasses to shield my eyes from the glare of the light that surrounds his essence on the planet where he now lives. He "didn't die," as explained in the movie, Men In Black, "he just went home." Address unknown.

Having the information from Mojo Nixon, that, "Elvis is everywhere," I was able to 'go cat go', and return from sender, with the knowledge that his highness was more human than he was allowed to be.

ALOHA FROM HAWAII via SATELLITE is Smithstonian history. It is from a January 1973 show that was engineered to reach around the globe. Due to space age technology that cost over 2 million dollars to organize and produce. Elvis never once did a show outside the USA, so an estimated 1.5 billion hungry people from 40 countries viewed the show in real time. The funny thing is it wasn't broadcasted to American audiences till April of that same year.

It's all well documented in the scores of books out there, so rehashing the story about Colonel Tom Parker, The Memphis Mafia, the descent into drug addiction and the splendid isolation would be boring. I will say that this show and album was designed as a comeback and to kick-start Elvis into the next stage of his career: When he and his music meant something again. Colonel Tom had new horizons to explore and Captain Elvis needed boats. Sadly, it would be the last notable thing he ever did because once he squeezed into the jumpsuit and karate kicked it on stage it became a comfortable parody that made money honey. Why stretch yourself when the material is made to stretch with the expanding waistline.

The album was released in February of 1973, not a month out from the actual show and it went to straight number one on the charts and on to sell millions. Elvis was back and was singing songs and performing onstage and not in lousy movies. You could say this was a companion set from the Madison Square Garden album from 1972, with almost

Live Album Review

the same show, with the interchanging of some oldies, that was a big seller as well. It was clear, if it said, "Elvis" it would move.

Sprach Zarathustra opens with the full band and orchestra playing to welcome Elvis' grand entrance to sing, "*See See Rider.*" It's rock and roll with a large band that includes James Burton on guitar. I know, you know there's the basic drums, bass and piano, as well as the Sweet Inspirations and the Jordanaires Quartet on vocals and an orchestra and conductor. It all feels like The Tonight Show Band backing up his highness with little margin for error or any off script shenanigans, thank ya very much.

Good songs? A big hunk. "*Burning Love*" is his recent hit and being positioned early shows this show is going to be good. "*Something*" is a song from that British group that got to meet Elvis in his royal chambers. Did John really jam with Elvis? Some sources say Elvis wasn't a fan of The Beatles but a good song is a good song. I do have to wonder why the low brass playing on this sounds like flatulence. It's clear as a bell and if on purpose or not, it's funny.

"*You Gave Me A Mountain*" is a powerful performance. It would appear that this type of song would be suited to Elvis and his mature audience. It works, but it ain't rock and rock. Elvis did have a great set of pipes. He could growl with the best of them but also sing ever so sweetly.

"*Steamroller*", for me, is the best song from this show. Elvis sounds as if he was made for this style of blues. He effortlessly glides through it with some real attitude. "I'm a napalm bomb baby," indeed. Who cares what those peace-nicks think? Elvis knows what Americans make up his audi-ence. A little more of this action if you please.

"*My Way*" would give Ol Blue Eyes a run for his money with the full band production and emotional vocal perfor-mance. "*Love Me*" has the over-the-top hip shaking, and the crowd loves it. If the 'pelvis' asks to be treated like a fool, then he'll act like one, even if it's in jest to bygone exploits.

I'm not sure why "*Johnny B Goode*" is necessary. It can almost be biographical, but it's not his song. Elvis had great songs from the early, pre-Army days that he could have done instead. Nobody ever asks me.

"*It's Over*" is moving and sweet and sets up the stripped down but quick version of "Blue Suede Shoes" the almost country reading of "*I'm So Lonesome I Could Cry*" (the saddest song I've ever heard). "*I Can't Stop Loving You*"and "*Hound Dog*" (the shortest song here) that includes some wah- wah guitar. That's real cool man, real cool. This is a concert guaranteed to not disappoint. "What Now", "*Fe-ver*", "*Welcome To My World*" (yawn) and "*Suspicious Minds*" that's played at breakneck speed. "I hope this suit doesn't tear up," out Jaggers, "you wouldn't want me trousers to fall

Live Album Review

down."

Elvis introduces everyone on stage before singing, *"I'll Remember You"* which is another one of the songs patterned to touch the gray haired crowd. I never got into that kind of song and felt it belonged to the crooners but hey, Tom Jones sang this stuff too, so try to be everything to everyone. I guess. *"American Trilogy"* would continue this vibe and in 1973. Of course a white man from the south could get away with singing songs about Dixie.

The rock and roll oldie of *"Big Hunk Of Love"* is as gritty as things will get on this night. It's noticeable that this is what The Beatles cut their teeth on when young. I can hear what Elvis did back in the 50s, not only made him rich, but influenced scores of artists that were to follow.

"Can't Help Falling In Love" is a perfect ending to the evening's festivities, even though Elvis would return later to record songs without an audience for later release.

He does, from a place of respect. He does a quick run through of *"Blue Hawaii"* before saying good night and, "Thank ya very much."

That phrase has become part of his legend and some claim he didn't really say it all that much. I counted, and he said it twenty times during this show. You can smile about it or shake your head at the show-biz hype. Myself, I hear with fondness and a deep sense of loss. Whatever Elvis meant to you, he mattered and still does to millions. He went beyond celebrity and became a part of American culture. It ended up killing him at too young an age, but without him, music we love today would have gone through another door and traveled a different road and may have come out sideways.

For that I say to Elvis, "Thank ya very much."

Live Album Review

FREE LIVE!

BY: FREE

There are better live concerts from Free out there but this was the official release in 1971. "*Alright Now*" starts things off, and it's curious why a band with that one hit song would start their show with it, but they did. It doesn't really matter. Paul Rodgers' voice and Paul Kossoff's guitar are magic regardless of what song they are playing. "*Be My Friend*" and "*Mister Big*" are the two tracks on this set that literally hypnotize the listener.

The trademark Simon Kirke heavy hitting starts before Kossoff plays a dirty guitar riff. A weaving bass line from Andy Fraser gets the groove right before Paul Rodgers starts singing the most expressive, white boy blues by anyone. Guitar solos by Kossoff aren't free-form improvisations, they're actual compositions and are integral to the song. This band was, to use an old cliche, "ahead of their time." Kossoff would pass away in 1976 and it's a wonder what great things musically he would have done had he survived. He was 5 feet tall but played like a giant. He had the gift. That and Paul Rodger's gifts are what make this album special. Free music has been covered by artists from Three Dog Night to Government Mule. The legacy lives on. Bad Company was a sanitized version of Free and more popular. As much as I like Mick Ralphs, and he would cite Kossoff as a main influence, the truth is the student will never be as good as the master. This album shows what a master can do, and it wasn't even that good of a performance.

LIVE! BULLET!

BY: BOB SEGER

There are many kinds of live albums. Those released to fulfill a contractual obligation, those to get some quick cash, those for the fans and those to gather in a wider audience. LIVE BULLET by Bob Seger, falls in the last category. Released in 1976, this show is from his stomping ground of Detroit. He had a regional following at the time and this live set helped introduce him to people outside the midwest USA. Seger was smart to include the good songs from his studio albums, *"Beautiful Loser"*, *"Nutbush City Limits"*, *"Get Out Of Denver"*, *"Kathmandu"*, *"Rambin' Gamblin Man"* and *"Turn The Page"*. It's *"Turn The Page"* that captured the uninitiated.

The sax solo on that is one of those defining moments in an artists' career. Those exist throughout rock and roll. Instantly recognizable The opening riff to *"Sweet Child Of Mine"* or the cowbell intro to *"Honky Tonk Women"* or the *"I Am Iron Man"* to the Black Sabbath classic. I'm sure you can count off thousands of your own. The point being the sax solo to *"Turn The Page"* is Bob Seger's defining moment.

This complete album is a favorite memory for me. The music is no-frills, meat and potatoes rock and roll. It's designed to reach the people in the cheap seats as well as the people in the front row. The east coast had Springsteen, who was being hyped as the next Dylan that had his finger on the pulse of the common man. Well, the Midwest was proud of their own common man hero and this live set showed everyone why. Springsteen was ambiguous at times, where Seger wore his heart on his sleeve and was dedicated. He worked every bit as hard on stage as 'The Boss'. The album, *NIGHT MOVES*, released later would eventually break Seger into the big time. This album paved the way.

Live Album Review

BAND OF GYPSIES

BY: JIMI HENDRIX

Released six months before he would leave us, this live set from Jimi Hendrix and his Band of Gypsys would be the last record he would personally oversee. Taken from performances at The Fillmore East, Jimi was playing with new people and, according to some, moving in a new musical direction. I don't hear it. It sounds similar to what he was doing with The Experience. Granted, few selections from those shows made it onto this set, but that's because the record company wanted new material. The opening song, "*Who Knows*" is a classic Hendrix riff. He does some scattered singing before his Strat blasts off. It's great, and it's Jimi Hendrix, but I'm not hearing jazz or funk fusion, as some claim. I'm hearing acid rock, but maybe my ears are bad.

"*Machine Gun*" is basically the same song as the former song, with a few differences. In fact, the only two typical songs would be the Buddy Miles compositions of "*Them Changes*" and "*We Gotta Live Together*". Now these two show a different side to Hendrix because he doesn't sing the lead vocal and plays more of a supporting role as a musician. If the band had a perfect opportunity to funk things up, it would be on these two numbers, but they don't.

Don't get me wrong, this is not a disappointing listen. It's what the audience, at the time, expected from Hendrix. They wanted him to provide the music for the trip they were taking. He provided it well and his approach would be the template for the next generation of rock guitar players to follow.

Live Album Review

Edward Milano

Live Album Review

ALIVE SHE CRIED

BY: THE DOORS

Twelve years after Jim Morrison died, the Doors were still making money. I do commend their restraint and respect by not flooding the market with anything they could find with Jim Morrison on it. The myth regarding the live set, ALIVE SHE CRIED, is that there was a renewed interest in the band due to the movie, 'Apocalypse Now.' Five years between that film and this set is a long time to prepare a 30 minute, live album, so I doubt that was the reason. It's about the money and giving people a great document of The Doors in concert.

There was a double live album in 1970, *ABSOLUTELY LIVE* that was not so well received because it lacked hits. The 1983 release, *ALIVE SHE CRIED* has some better known songs, as well as some Jim Morrison poetry and theater. What's nice is there's just enough of both to make it a listen that is heavy on glee and light on the darkness.

"Gloria" opens this album and it was one of the early

songs the band learned and performed. It's a straight-for-ward reading, with the main riff carrying the performance, as Jim sings, yells and has the band slow it down so he can go off into a pornographic tale of him and a (probably under-age) girl, at her house, where the parents are gone. This is the stuff of legend where Jim Morrison is pushing the enve-lope. The band is locked in and the combination of Robbie Kreiger's blues licks, the jazz drumming of John Densmore and the carnival organ of Ray Manzarek, created a sound that is unmistakingly, The Doors.

"*Light My Fire*" is almost 10 minutes of one of the top 10 rock songs from the 1960's. Ray starts getting weird, in the middle and breaks into some Phantom of the Opera, organ noises. A poetry reading from Jim, "*The Graveyard Poem*" was dubbed into the middle section. It wasn't part of this actual performance but it works and gives the listener a chance to get a feel for Jim Morrison, the serious artist. The drawback, for me, is the hard-headed resolve of Manzarek to play the keyboard bass instead of having a real bass play-er onstage to fill things out. If Robbie isn't running through some bass patterns on his guitar, Ray is handling the bass duties on his keyboards while also playing the melodious accompaniment. Just because you have the talent to do this doesn't mean you should.

"*You Make Me Real*" is a blues rocker from *MORRI-*

Live Album Review

SON HOTEL and it appears the Doors are focusing on rock and blues on this set, which is the direction Robbie Kreiger was pushing the band to do more of. This is the only performance from this album where Jim and the band play things straight and not go too far off the path.

"*The WASP (Texas Radio and the Big Beat)*" and "*Love Me Two Times*" are combined, which gives life to Jim's spoken word act.

John Sebastian joins the band on "*Little Red Rooster*" and provides some credible, blues harmonica. This is the best song from the album and Robbie Kreiger is a serious, blues aficionado. He didn't receive the acclaim, that was probably due him, for his guitar work with The Doors and that's just the way the cards fell. He and John Sebastian chop heads and Ray even takes a turn with his carnival organ. It's The Doors, stepping out of Morrison's shadow and showing they weren't just his backing band.

"*Moonlight Mile*", which has "*Horse Latitudes*" included, is a nice listen to conclude this album, that I feel is perfect, as is ,and didn't need anymore or any less. It's the band rocking with Morrison, who is in good voice, with just enough poetry and narcissistic attitude to give a condensed example of what The Doors were as a musical entity and the front man that launched a thousand trips.

Edward Milano

Live Album Review

Edward Milano

Live Album Review

Printed in the USA
CPSIA information can be obtained
at www.ICGtesting.com
LVHW012304100824
787895LV00011B/266